Totally Awesome Devotional for Preteen Boys

43 Engaging Bible Lessons for Spiritual Growth, Christ-Based Confidence, and Faith to Handle Life's Challenges

Julian Locke

To my lovely Wife, without your unwavering love and support, I could not have written this book. I am blessed to have you by my side.

To my son Noah, who I give thanks to God for the blessing you are, and your boundless energy for adventure. May this book be a guide for you and help you grow in faith and wisdom. Jesus is truly the greatest gift I can share with you. He is totally Awesome!.

To my church family, I am truly blessed to share this journey with each of you. I am deeply grateful to the many friends who have offered encouragement and wise counsel along the way. May we, together with our families, continue to treasure Jesus more each day.

***

Contents

Introduction

"Why bother with another book? I'd rather watch YouTube."

I get it, really. Another book? And a devotional, no less? It sounds like a snooze fest is waiting to happen, right? But hang on—what if I told you this isn't just any book? This is about diving into life's biggest adventure with the best coach (God) beside you. And yeah, not being an expert or a pastor might sound sus, but here's the scoop: I'm just like you, figuring out this wild ride with a little help from above. I am no expert, and I mess up all the time. But I know this for real: God is super awesome, no joke.

Think about playing Fortnite or Minecraft. Now, imagine trying to survive those games blindfolded. Pretty chaotic, huh? That's sort of like trying to navigate life without understanding how much God loves you. It's like missing out on the most important goal. So, here's this book, aiming to be your little signboard, showing you the right starting position so you won't have to fumble around the map blindfolded. It's not the ultimate guide—that's the Bible—but it's like a sneak peek of how awesome God is. Just a taste to get you hooked and keep you chasing that epic goodness in your life's adventure game. And hopefully, once you know it tastes great, you can experience the full-course meal by going back to the Bible.

This isn't your everyday devotional. Nope. It's packed with fun facts that'll blow your mind and activities that won't make you yawn. And check out the "Skill Checks" to test what you've learned along the way, and the "Save Your Game Plan" section where you can jot down your thoughts and lock in your progress as you level up in this faith adventure. We're talking about real stuff here—like handling school stress, dealing with bullies, and even tackling what to do when your family dynamics get as glitchy as a bad internet connection.

Right off the bat, why not try this? Grab a piece of paper and jot down what you think about God or devotionals. No essays, no right or wrong answers—just your honest thoughts. It's cool, I'll wait.

Got it? Great! Now, as we flip through these pages together, keep that paper handy. You might find your thoughts changing, or hey, they might stay the same. But give it a shot. What's there to lose?

There's no rush here. You can tackle a topic each day or take it slow and do one each week. Maybe even go through it with your parents. What matters most is that you really take in these awesome lessons at your own pace. And despite what you might think, this journey could turn out to be pretty epic. You're not just reading a book; you're stepping up your game in life, faith, and understanding that, yeah, God is totally AWESOME. And He's got your back, through thick and thin, just like the best squad mate you could ever have.

So, why not give this a go? Who knows, you might just find that diving into God's word is like discovering the coolest new game feature you didn't know existed. Ready to hit start and play the game of life with some pro tips? Let's roll!

***

Building Faith Foundations

LISTEN UP! THIS FIRST chapter is our foundation, like the base of a super tall tower. Everything from Chapter 2 onward is built on this. If the base isn't strong, the whole thing will come crashing down like a stack of cards. Some of you might already know these stories, but that's even better. The more we reinforce it, the stronger we'll be at facing this adventure called life. Are you ready? Let's do this!

Alright, let's start with something pretty epic—how everything began! Nope, not just the start of your favorite video game or the first episode of that show you binge-watched last weekend. We're talking about the beginning of everything. Ever wonder how all this stuff around us came to be? Trees, animals, Wi-Fi... Well, maybe not Wi-Fi, but you get the idea. It all started somewhere, right?

Chapter 1
Creation and Me: Finding My Place in God's World

GENESIS 1:31 (NIV):

"God saw all that he had made, and it was very good. And there was evening, and there was morning—the sixth day."

Ever booted up a new game like Minecraft and found yourself starting from scratch? You've got no tools, no shelter—nothing. But bit by bit, you gather resources, build your base, and soon you've got a whole world created just from a few simple blocks. That's a bit like what God did, but on a massive scale, and let's just say He didn't need any tutorial or walkthrough to get it right the first time.

When you dive into the story of Genesis, it's not just a tale of how things came to be. It's about God's mega project—creating the universe, Earth, animals, and yeah, humans too (that's us!). And He did it all with a purpose. Every mountain, every river, every creepy crawly that makes you go "Eww!" was made with intention. Think of God as the ultimate game designer; only His graphics are real life, and His gameplay is the world we live in.

Now, how does this all connect to you? Ever thought about why you're here or what your purpose is? The Bible says we're created to make a big deal about God and enjoy Him forever. That's when we're the happiest, most on point, and feel totally at home. Plus, just like every block in Minecraft serves a purpose, so do you. God designed you uniquely—your humor, your talents, your weird obsession with collecting things—each part of you was crafted for a reason. You're not just some random player; you're a key character in this world with your own part to play.

That means you're not only one-of-a-kind, but you're also super valuable. Imagine you create a character in a game—you spend hours tweaking it, making it special and different from all the others. In fact, there's a special ID on it to show that only you made it. It might even look a bit like you. You're so proud of it; you're not gonna just delete it when it doesn't work right. You spend time fixing it and improving it. Kinda like that; there's a special value that God puts in the people He created. That means you, your mom, dad, friends, and even that funny guy across the street. Not only that, God made you in His 'image.' Just like that special ID, you're a reflection of the Creator. God is so proud of it; He said it was very good! Think about that—we were created with great value, and it is VERY good. He's not gonna just throw you away.

But hey, with great power comes great responsibility, right? That's where stewardship comes into play. Just like you wouldn't trash your own room (I hope not, at least), you wouldn't want to trash the world either. Simple things like recycling that soda can or turning off the water while you brush your teeth are like the daily quests in your favorite games, except this helps level up the planet.

And think about this—when you create worlds in games, you're mirroring what God did with our world. That creativity is a big deal; it's a reflection of God's image. So next time you're building something awesome in your game, remember, you've got that creative spark because God put it there. And just like you respect and protect your digital creations, we ought to do the same with God's creation. Next time you're out in the park or chilling in your backyard, take a second to look around and appreciate the insane graphics God hooked us up with—no update needed, always HD, 100% immersive. Now, that's what I call a divine design!

Prayer

Dear God, thank You for the beauty and wonder of Your creation. Help me to also see and be amazed that you created everything including me and it was very good. Help me to remember to care for the Earth and all its creatures as a reflection of Your love. Amen.

Cool Activity

Here's a quick quest for you: Grab a notebook and jot down three ways you interact with nature every day and how you can turn those interactions into ways of taking care of what God has created. Maybe it's biking to school to cut down on car pollution, or perhaps it's saving electricity by powering down your gaming console when not in use. Whatever it is, write it down. You might not get XP points, but you're leveling up for Team Earth!

Skill check

> Think about something you're really proud of creating,
> whether in a game or real life. How does knowing you're
> made in God's image make you feel about your own
> uniqueness and value?

....

....

....

....

Save Your Game Plan

....

....

....

....

Chapter 2
Sin and Forgiveness: Understanding Mistakes and Grace

ROMANS 3:23 (NIV):

"For all have sinned and fall short of the glory of God."

Ever had one of those days where everything you touch seems to go spectacularly wrong? Maybe you fibbed about your score in a video game to seem cooler to your friends, or perhaps you hid a bad report card because the thought of showing your parents made your stomach do backflips. It feels like you've hit a glitch in your personal gameplay, doesn't it? Well, in God's vocab, these mess-ups are called 'sin'. And here's the kicker—sin isn't just about breaking rules; it's anything that puts a wedge between you and God.

And this isn't just any small problem, like a busted Wi-Fi signal or a connection problem. It's a massive hole, so big that it's impossible to get out of. Not just you, but everyone. How? I wasn't even there! I know, right? But remember when God created the world? He made Adam and Eve. Think of them not just as the first people but as the reps for all people, kinda like how a team leader represents the whole team. What they do affects all of us. And sadly... they messed up. They ate the fruit that God told them NOT to.

Now, imagine you're in a tight spot where you've let someone down. Maybe you snapped at your little brother or forgot to do your part of a group project. Imagine what that does to your relationship. The once close, valuable, free, happy, and awesome relationship is all messed up. Seriously, 'cause if we're being real, we know we mess up sometimes. We're all in that massive hole, and we need saving.

But you might be thinking, 'I'm a good person, right? I do my homework, and I don't hang out with the bad kids. Why am I sinful?' Well, God is super holy, way beyond anything we can imagine. He's perfect and wants us to be perfect too. Even if we don't do really bad stuff like murder, we still mess up and fall short of what He expects. It's like aiming for a perfect score in a game and missing by just a little—you still didn't make it. As it says in Romans 3:23, we all mess up and fall short. That's what sin is: not hitting God's perfect standard.

But here's the good news—God's got something awesome up His divine sleeve, and it's called grace. Think of grace as the ultimate reset button. Messed up? Hit reset. Feeling down about it? Hit reset. It's always there, and it never runs out. It doesn't matter how smart you are or how good or bad you've been. You might even feel like you deserve to be grounded for life! No matter what, God's grace is always there for you. Always, 24/7. No cap.

But here's the thing: unlike resetting a game where everything goes back to normal instantly, grace doesn't just sweep things under the rug. It rebuilds trust and fixes relationships, making things right in a way that lasts. It's serious stuff because, unlike a video game, the consequences in real life aren't just a 'Game Over' screen—they affect real hearts and real relationships. But how does God deal with these consequences? Stay tuned for the next chapter...Spoiler Alert: GOD SEND JESUS

So, here's a real-life application for you. Next time you find yourself on the 'I really messed up' side of things, take a deep breath and remember it's not the end of the world. Own up to what you've done, and hit that divine reset button of grace.

Prayer

Dear Lord, I know that I make mistakes and sometimes choose the wrong path. Thank You for Your endless forgiveness and grace that always brings me back to You. Help me to turn from my sins and grow closer to You each day. Amen.

***

"Sin and Grace Balloon Pop"

Materials: Balloons, small paper, pens, container, pins, Bibles.

1. **Write Sins:**

   - Participants anonymously write sins on paper.

   - Collect papers in a container.

2. **Balloon Filling:**

   - Place one paper in each balloon, then inflate.

3. **Activity:**

   - Scatter balloons (representing sin).

   - Take turns popping balloons and reading sins aloud.

4. **Discuss:**

   - Talk about sin and its consequences.

   - Read Bible verses on forgiveness.

   - Discuss how Jesus frees us from sin like popping the balloon releases the paper.

***

Skill check

> In a game, missing a perfect score by even a little bit means you didn't win. How does this compare to how we all 'fall short' of God's perfect standard? Why do you think God's grace is so important for us, even when we try our best?

....

....

....

....

Save Your Game Plan

....

....

....

....

Chapter 3
Salvation Quest: Jesus, the Ultimate Hero

JOHN 3:16-17 (NIV):

"For God so loved the world that he gave his one and only Son, that whoever believes in him shall not perish but have eternal life. For God did not send his Son into the world to condemn the world, but to save the world through him.

Imagine you're stuck in an epic video game, cornered with no weapons left, and the mega boss is closing in. Game over, right? Not quite. Just when things look the bleakest, in swoops the ultimate superhero—let's just call him Super Savior! He's not just any hero. He doesn't just save the day; he changes the entire game. Now, let's swap that controller for a Bible because this isn't the plot of the latest gaming blockbuster. This is the story of Jesus, and dude, it's the ultimate heroic saga.

So, picture this: Jesus, a carpenter from Nazareth, steps onto the scene. But he's no ordinary guy 'cause, well, God sent him. He comes with superpowers like healing the sick with just a touch, calming storms with a command, and yep, even bringing people back from the dead. But here's the kicker—his most epic showdown wasn't against aliens or monsters; it was against sin and death itself. And check out John 3:17, actually, God could have every right to condemn the world, but he did not. He sent His Son, Jesus, to fix the huge gap in our relationship caused by sin. Because if something is broken, you need to pay the price. Think about it: if you broke something at the store, you might be sorry, but your dad still needs to pay for what you broke. Being sorry does not piece together the broken plate on the floor.

What price did Jesus pay for us? It wasn't just like paying for something we broke; it was way bigger—He paid with His life. Seriously, our death. Jesus died instead of us because He loves us that much. When Jesus died on the cross and then came back three days later, it was like the ultimate boss battle, and guess what? He won. The price is paid, and there are no more penalties. The gap between us and God is gone.

Now, let's talk about why this matters to you. Think about your favorite superhero. Maybe someone who dashes around saving the world, always there just in the nick of time. Jesus is kinda like that, but even cooler because what he did goes beyond just saving the day. He offers us a rescue from something way bigger—sin's penalties. It's like being in a rough game where you keep getting hit, and suddenly, you've got unlimited health because Super Savior took the hits for you. Because of Jesus, we can face life knowing we're not alone and that ultimate victory is already ours. Never again will there be a wedge in the relationship between us and God. That's not just a game-changer; it's a life-changer.

And here's where it gets personal. Believing in what Jesus did isn't about just nodding along to a cool story; it's about trust. Like how you'd trust your buddy in a duo game to watch your back, trusting Jesus means leaning on him, knowing he's got your back, in-game and out. It's about living your life like you've got the ultimate savior on your side because, well, you do.

***

Prayer

Dear Jesus, thank You for being the greatest hero who came to save us all. Your love and sacrifice on the cross is amazing, and i cannot do it by myself. Help me to trust you and think about Jesus's love for me often. Because of him, i know i am not alone. Please help me share your story of salvation with others. Amen.

***

Interactive Challenge:
Write down some challenges you're facing (e.g., school stress, friendship issues). Reflect on how knowing Jesus is with you can change your approach.

Activity: "The Bridge to Salvation"
Materials: Open space, masking tape/chalk, cardboard/foam board, markers, Bible, index cards.

1. **Set Up:**

   - Mark two lines on the ground (one for humanity, one for God).

   - Create a "bridge" between them labeled "Jesus."

2. **Steps:**

   - Write a sin on an index card; place it between the lines as an obstacle.

   - Attempt to cross the gap without the bridge—it's difficult.

   - Explain that Jesus is the bridge that connects us to God.

***

Skill check

> Think about a time when you were in trouble and need-
> ed help. How does knowing that Jesus 'changed the
> game' for all of us by taking on sin and death make you
> feel about your relationship with Him?

....

....

....

....

Save Your Game Plan

....

....

....

....

Chapter 4

Prayer Power-Ups: Talking to God Like He's More Than Your Best Friend

PHILIPPIANS 4:6-7 (NIV):

"Do not be anxious about anything, but in every situation, by prayer and petition, with thanksgiving, present your requests to God. And the peace of God, which transcends all understanding, will guard your hearts and your minds in Christ Jesus."

Ever had a late-night chat with your best bud, just talking about whatever pops into your head, no filters, no fancy words needed? Well, praying's kinda like that, but imagine you're chatting with the ultimate best friend—God. No need to dress up your words or sound super formal; it's all about keeping it real. Think of prayer as your direct line to God, where you can talk about anything and everything. And I mean ANYTHING and in EVERY situation, as it says in Philippians 4:6. Yeah, He's really that approachable, and that's really reassuring.

And when you think about it, that's pretty incredible. With so many people talking to Him every day, you'd think He'd be too busy, like managing a giant chat room or making sure everything runs smoothly. But actually, nope, you can still approach Him. You might think He's too important or too powerful to care about your small prayers. But nope, you can still approach Him. No matter what, you have the most secure direct messaging with God. Nothing can change that.

So, what's up with all the different ways people pray? Well, it's kind of like having different chats depending on what's going on. For starters, there's thanksgiving, which is like sending a thank-you text after your friend hooked you up with a cool game or shared their lunch when you forgot yours. It's about appreciating the good stuff God's tossed your way. Then there's supplication, which is a fancy way of saying you're asking God for something—like maybe some courage to try out for the school play or help with a tough math test coming up. Intercession is when you're looking out for your buddies, your family, or even your annoying little brother. It's asking God to give them a hand.

Now, making prayer a regular part of your day might sound like a lot, but it's totally doable. Think of it as turning small moments into mini-chat sessions with God. Stuck in the car on the way to school? Shoot a quick prayer for your day or your family. Watching your team play and hoping for a win? Whisper a quick prayer for good performance or sportsmanship. And remember, it's not just the best DM ever—it's also the most powerful.

And here's the kicker—don't get bummed if it feels weird at first or if you forget a day or two. Like any epic game, prayer takes practice. The more you chat with God, the more natural it'll feel. Set reminders if you have to, maybe right before bed or first thing when you wake up. Think of it like scheduling your gaming sessions; you wouldn't miss those, right? So, setting a regular time for prayer can help make it a no-brainer part of your day. And eventually, when you come to know and enjoy how awesome God is, you'll actually want to do it. It won't be a hassle or a chore anymore.

Remember, this whole prayer gig isn't about racking up points for the number of words you say or making sure you've got the fanciest phrases. It's about keeping it real with God, knowing He's up for a chat anytime. Whether you're on top of the world or the game's got you down, He's there, ready to listen. And the cool part? He never gets tired of hearing from you. So, keep that line open, keep the chats rolling, and watch how these conversations with God start to change your game, one prayer at a time. Remember, it's like calling in the best kind of reinforcement—you might not see Him, but God's always got your back, powering you up for whatever lies ahead.

Prayer

Dear God, thank You for always being there to listen to me, like the best friend I could ever have and so much more. Help me to come to You with all my thoughts, worries, and joys, knowing that You care deeply for me. Teach me to trust in our conversations and to find peace in Your presence. Amen.

Cool Activity

Here's a fun idea: try making a prayer jar. Grab any old jar and some paper. Every time something bugs you or you feel super thankful about something, jot it down and pop it in the jar. It's like keeping a log of all the things you want to chat about with God. Then, whenever you're feeling up for it, pull out a note and have a chat about it. Plus, over time, you can look back and see all the ways God's been part of your game.

Skill check

> When you talk to God in prayer, do you find it easy or difficult to keep it real? What are some things you could start chatting with God about, just like you would with your best friend?

....

....

....

....

Save Your Game Plan

....

....

....

....

Chapter 5
Church Vibes: Why Bother Going?

ACTS 2:42 (NIV):

"They devoted themselves to the apostles' teaching and to fellowship, to the breaking of bread and to prayer."

Ever wondered why people get super pumped about going to church? It might seem like just another building with a bunch of people hanging out, kind of like going to school or hitting the mall. But trust me, it's way more than that. Think of church not just as a place, but as a team—yeah, like your favorite sports team, where everyone has a unique role to play. Every player matters, whether you're the star quarterback or the guy who makes sure everyone gets a high-five. In church, whether you're the lead singer in the choir or the dude passing out programs, you're part of something bigger.

But here's the kicker: being part of a church means you're part of a family. Think about that—the awesome God knew we couldn't do this alone, so He gave us a family. Not just any family, but a big, sprawling, sometimes messy or annoying, but totally awesome family. And like any family, you've got people from all sorts of backgrounds and stories, coming together under one roof. And what do families do? As it says in Acts 2:42, they live life together. They learn, grow, eat, and pray together, all because of God's love for them. It's like having home-field advantage in every game because you're surrounded by fans who are rooting for you and totally get you. And just like a home game, it feels right because you're exactly where you belong.

You know how leveling up in games feels pretty awesome because you see your progress right there on the screen? Going to church can feel like that too. It's where you level up spiritually. You learn new things, face challenges with a team, and even find mentors who've been in your shoes and have maps for the tricky parts of the game of life. They're like the experienced players who've been around and know how to dodge the tough stuff or climb to new heights.

Church is also about getting your hands dirty—yeah, in a good way! Ever helped out at a food drive or played guitar in the worship band? That's church in action. It's about pitching in, helping out, and sometimes stepping out of your comfort zone. It's where you can try new things like leading a prayer, helping with tech stuff, or even just giving someone a listening ear. And the cool part? You get to see the difference you make, right there, right then. It's about being a light in sometimes dark places, showing God's love through action.

Now, imagine playing a multiplayer game where everyone seriously gets you. They've got your back whether you're nailing it or when you totally biff it. That's church. It's where you meet folks who understand the faith journey you're on because, dude, they're walking it with you. They're the squad you rally with when things get tough, and let's be real, sometimes you need that backup. Plus, it's not just about hanging out; it's about growing stronger together, learning more about God, and yeah, getting that spiritual boost that we all kinda crave, even if we don't admit it.

So, why go to church? Because it's where you can be real. It's where you can grow, laugh, maybe sing way off-key, and learn stuff about God that you never thought about before. It's meant to be where you're valued, no matter your high score or how often you've stumbled. And yes, sometimes there are people you might not get along with, but that can happen everywhere, not just in the church. It's about imperfect people loving each other. And just maybe, you'll find that going to church isn't just about showing up; it's about belonging, growing, and being part of a team that cheers you on, no matter what. So next Sunday, or whenever your church doors swing open, why not jump in? You might just find it's exactly where you need to be, ready to high-five you into the next chapter of your adventure. And who knows? You might even have some fun along the way.

***

Prayer

Dear Lord, thank You for the gift of the church and the community of believers. Help me to understand the importance of gathering with others to worship, learn, and grow in faith. Remind me that through church, I can find support and encouragement. Amen.

Church Bingo

Objective:
Have fun exploring the special aspects of church life!

Materials:
You'll need Bingo cards, markers or pens, small prizes (optional), and a list of church activities to call out.

Instructions:

1. **Prepare Cards:**

   - Create a 5x5 grid on each card and fill the squares with church-related activities like Worship, Prayer, and Fellowship.

2. **Explain the Game:**

   - Give each player a card and marker. The leader will call out activities from the list, and players mark their squares if they have the activity.

3. **Play:**

   - The first person to complete a row, column, or diagonal shouts "Bingo!" and wins.

Skill check

How is being part of a church family, all connected by Jesus' love, like being on a team? What's one thing you can do to help your church team grow stronger together

....

....

....

....

Save Your Game Plan

....

....

....

....

Chapter 6
Daily Bible Quest: Your Ultimate Treasure Hunt

PSALM 119:105 (NIV):

"Your word is a lamp to my feet and a light to my path."

Hey there, adventurer! Have you ever dreamed of finding hidden treasure? Well, guess what? You've got a treasure map right at your fingertips – it's called the Bible! Let's explore why diving into this daily treasure hunt is totally worth it.

Think about trying to find a treasure without a map. Pretty impossible, right? The Bible is like God's treasure map, packed with everything you need to understand who God is, who you are, what the big problem is, and how to solve it. Without it, we're just wandering around. But with it, we get the full picture and all the clues to live an epic life. As it says in Psalm 119:105, God's word is a 'light' and 'lamp'; it shows us the way so we don't get lost and leads us to the greatest treasure ever.

Maybe you're thinking, "I've learned a lot about the Bible in Sunday school. Why do I need to read it every day?" Imagine watching only the teasers of your favorite adventure movies like Avengers, Harry Potter, or Spider-Man. You'd miss out on all the epic twists and turns! Reading the Bible regularly helps you see the whole adventure, not just the highlights.

Let's break down this amazing story:

It all starts with God creating the world and everything in it. Everything was perfect, and we were made to enjoy and be with God.

Then came the problem – sin. It's like the bad guy in the story. Sin separated us from God and messed up the perfect world He created.

The Old Testament is filled with the story of the people of Israel trying to love and obey God. They had some high points, but they also failed a lot. It's like the build-up to the climax in any great story.

And then, the most epic part – Jesus arrives! He lived a perfect life and died for our sins. His resurrection is the ultimate victory over sin and death.

After Jesus ascended to heaven, His disciples continued the mission. They spread the good news and awaited the day when Jesus will return.

The story isn't over yet. We're still waiting for that happy ending where Jesus returns and God's kingdom is fully realized on earth as it is in heaven.

The coolest part? We're part of this amazing story! It's real life, and by reading the Bible, we get to see our place in God's incredible plan. But let's be real: life can be like a tough quest with lots of challenges. It's easy to forget how awesome God is when things get rough. That's why reading the Bible and praying every day is like finding daily treasure. It reminds you of God's love, gives you strength, and helps you face anything that comes your way. Plus, we're made to love, enjoy, and follow God. There's no better way to do that than diving into His word every day.

Prayer

"Dear God, thank you for giving us your word as a treasure map for our lives. Help me to read it daily, understand it, and enjoy it. Let it guide my steps and give me strength for every adventure. Amen."

***

Bible Treasure Hunt

Objective:

Teach the value of daily Bible reading through a fun treasure hunt.

Materials:

Bibles, treasure map, clue cards, small treasures, pens, paper, final treasure box.

Preparation:

Create a map and clue cards with Bible verses. Hide clues and treasures.

Activity:

1. **Introduction:**

   ○ Explain the Bible as a life-guiding treasure map.

2. **Teams:**

   ○ Divide into teams with a Bible and notepad.

3. **Hunt:**

   ○ Start with a clue to Genesis 1:1. Teams find verses and move to the next clue.

4. **Final Treasure:**

   ○ Follow clues to a final prize reinforcing the lesson.

5. **Debrief:**

   ○ Discuss and close with a prayer.

Skill check

> Why do you think reading the Bible every day is important, even if you've heard the stories before? How can it help you find your place in God's big adventure

....

....

....

....

Save Your Game Plan

....

....

....

....

Dealing with Daily Drama

Ever felt like your school is just a big ol' multiplayer arena where everyone's scrambling to finish quests and sometimes, stepping on each other's toes? Yep, navigating through school life can feel like dodging banana peels in Mario Kart—unexpected, tricky, and sometimes downright wild. But hey, here's the good news: just like any game, there are strategies to not just survive, but totally rock it. Let's dive into the first boss level of school life—dealing with conflicts.

Chapter 7
PvP Showdowns: Handling Conflict with Grace

ROMANS 12:18 (NIV):

"If it is possible, as far as it depends on you, live at peace with everyone."

So, what's the deal with conflicts? Well, imagine you're in a Minecraft server, and someone just blew up the awesome castle you've been building for weeks. Ouch, right? That burning feeling of frustration is pretty much the start of a conflict. Conflicts happen because we're all different, and we see things from our own viewpoints. Sometimes, what you think is a cool joke, someone else might find it upsetting. It's like when two gamers try to play a co-op game but can't agree on the strategy—everyone has their own idea of how to win the game.

Take Paul and Barnabas in the Bible—two seriously cool dudes who teamed up for some epic missionary quests. But even they had a major fallout over whether to take a buddy (John Mark) on their next adventure. Both had good intentions, but they just couldn't agree. It shows that even the best of us can clash, but hey, it's not the end of the story. And guess what? Eventually, Paul resolves the conflict about John Mark. He eventually asked for him to come help him out! "Get John Mark and bring him with you to me, because he is helpful to me in my ministry" (2 Tim. 4:11)

Now, how do you sort out a mess like that? Well, let's talk godly game plans for peace. First up, forgiveness. It's like hitting the reset button on your console. Doesn't undo the past, but it clears the stage for a fresh start. Next, reconciliation.

This is where you and the other guy work it out and get back on the same team. It might mean swallowing your pride like a bitter power-up pill, but what are the results? Totally worth it. And sometimes, you both might still not agree. That doesn't mean you can't be friends or that you are a hater. You can still enjoy meals, study together, and play together. Remember, even if things don't work out, you are still loved by Jesus, and He forms who you are. You don't always have to agree with everyone. God's got your back.

But why must we be at 'peace' with others? Can't I just ignore them? Well, Romans 12:18 tells us to do our best to get along with everyone, especially in our church family. Let's not let little disagreements mess up the good vibes that come from God's love for us.

Speaking of peace, being a peacemaker doesn't mean letting everyone walk all over you like a doormat at the castle entrance. It's about standing your ground but doing it with respect, kindness, and always seeking to do what is right and good. And if things get too wild to handle on your own, like if the schoolyard scuffle turns into a full-blown boss battle, it's totally okay to tag in a grown-up. A teacher, counselor, or coach can help mediate, making sure everyone gets a fair shot at being heard.

And remember, every hero needs a good support crew. If you ever feel like you're stuck in a multiplayer match gone wrong, reach out. Talk to someone who can help you navigate the tricky levels. Whether it's a friend, a family member, or someone at school, having a team can make all the difference. So keep your head up, your heart open, and your game strong. Let's level up in handling those schoolyard scuffles like the champs we are!

***

Prayer

Dear God, sometimes I face conflicts and arguments that are hard to handle. Please give me the wisdom to respond with kindness and patience, and the strength to seek peace and understanding. Help me to be a peacemaker and to reflect Your love even in difficult situations. Amen.

***

Conflict Resolution Role-Play

Prepare Scenarios:

Create index cards with conflicts like:

Scenario 1: Sharing

"You and a friend want to use the same game console. What do you do?"

Scenario 2: Misunderstanding

"Your friend thinks you said something mean, but you didn't. How do you clear it up?"

Scenario 3: Bullying

"You see someone being bullied. How do you handle it?"

How to Play:

1. Draw a scenario card.

2. Think about how to resolve the conflict.

3. Act it out.

4. Discuss the resolution with the group.

***

Skill check

When you face conflicts, how can you be like a peace-maker and start fresh with forgiveness? What's one situation where you can try to make peace with someone, even if you don't agree?

....

....

....

....

Save Your Game Plan

....

....

....

....

Chapter 8
Finding Your Squad: How to Spot True Friends

PROVERBS 18:24 (NIV)

"One who has unreliable friends soon comes to ruin, but there is a friend who sticks closer than a brother."

Imagine you're in the ultimate team-up scenario in your favorite game. You're side by side with a buddy, facing down bosses, sharing power-ups, and covering each other's backs. That's the real-life version of a solid friendship. It's not just about hanging out and having fun—though those are definitely big pluses—it's about having someone who's got your back, no matter what level you're facing. Think about David and Jonathan in the Bible. These two were like legendary teammates. Jonathan even risked his own safety to help David out because he knew that's what true friends do—they protect and support each other, no matter the cost.

Now, you might be wondering: how do I spot a true friend in the wild? First off, a true friend cheers you on. If you're into drawing, they're hyped about your artwork. Into basketball? They're at your games, cheering whether you dunk or miss. They're the ones who encourage you in your faith, reminding you of God's cool plans for you when you're feeling low. Sometimes, they'll be honest and tell you when you messed up, even if you don't want to hear it. But here's the kicker—they don't lead you into trouble but help you steer clear of it. As it says in Proverbs 18:24, if they lead you to ruin, they aren't reliable.

Being a stellar friend isn't just about finding the right crew; it's about being the right crew member. It means throwing kindness around like confetti at a victory party. It's about being honest—even when it's about who ate the last slice of pizza—and supporting your pals, like giving a pep talk before a big test or listening when they've had a rough day. And here's a secret: when you're a good friend, you feel less pressured to fit into those crowded, often tricky social scenes. You're comfortable just being you with your small group of friends. You might even make others feel cool just by being themselves.

Friendships aren't about having a huge squad. Sometimes, just one or two good pals are all you need. It's like having a small but elite team where everyone plays their part perfectly. So, take a look around. Appreciate the friends who make your everyday kinda awesome, and be that friend to others, too. It's all about teaming up to win at the game of life, side by side, with the best teammates you could ask for. And remember, the best co-op adventures are the ones where everyone feels like they've got a player two who's truly got their back.

And finally, don't forget that Jesus is the ultimate best friend. He's got all the best qualities you could ever want in a buddy. He'll remind you of what He's done for you and keeps cheering you on, even now in Heaven. He can be real with you when you mess up, and His heart just aches to forgive and hug you every time. He will always be there. Even when everyone else lets you down, He never will. Even if you're the worst friend to Him and hate His guts, He still longs for you to come back. He really is the ultimate best friend.

***

Prayer

Dear God, thank You for the gift of friendship. Help me to recognize true friends who support, encourage, and lead me closer to You. Give me the wisdom to choose friends who reflect Your love and the courage to be a true friend to others. Amen.

***

Friendship Test Run

Think about tough times—who stuck by you? Those are your true friends.

Friendship Circle Challenge

1. **Prepare Cards:**

   - Write down friendship qualities (e.g., Kindness, Honesty, Loyalty) on separate cards.

2. **Explain the Game:**

   - Sit in a circle, shuffle the cards, and place them in the center.

   - Each person draws a card, reads the quality, and shares an example of how a friend showed it or how they can.

3. **Play the Game:**

   - Draw a card, share an example, and continue until everyone has participated.

***

Skill check

> How does knowing that Jesus is the ultimate best friend, who always has your back, help you in choosing and being a good friend? What's one way you can show your friends the same kind of loyalty and support?

....

....

....

....

Save Your Game Plan

....

....

....

....

Chapter 9
Peer Pressure: Standing Strong in Your Faith

ROMANS 12:2 (NIV)

"Do not conform to the pattern of this world, but be transformed by the renewing of your mind. Then you will be able to test and approve what God's will is—his good, pleasing and perfect will."

Ever felt like you're in a game where everyone's rushing to the next level, and you're just not sure if you want to follow the crowd? That's peer pressure, dude. It's like when everyone in your class decides to skip homework and wants you to do the same. It feels like you're standing at the edge of a cliff in a game, and all your buddies are jumping off, shouting for you to jump too. Peer pressure is powerful because nobody wants to be the odd one out, right? Everyone wants to be part of the squad.

Let's rewind to ancient times and check out a dude named Daniel. He was in a tough spot—captured, taken to a foreign land, and pressured to follow a lifestyle that went against his beliefs, including eating food that he wasn't cool with because it went against his faith. The stakes were high; it wasn't just about being unpopular—it was risky. But Daniel stood his ground. He knew munching on those royal meals wasn't right for him. It was about staying true to his faith, even when the pressure was cranked up to the max. Spoiler alert: Daniel sticks to his beliefs, and things turn out better than okay for him. He becomes a big-time advisor to the king. Talk about leveling up!

So, how do you deal with the peer pressure boss level in real life? David had this superpower to ignore peer pressure because he was all in on his faith in God. Even when everything around him fell apart, he knew God was still in control and would bring his people back together. He didn't worry about what others thought or did. He was confident that God had his back and believed that God's ways were always the best. Basically, he did what Romans 12:2 says, by not following the ways of the world around him and knowing God's ways are good, pleasing, and perfect.

And guess what? He wasn't flying solo; he had his three best buds with him. As you can see, choosing the right squad is crucial too. Surround yourself with buddies who respect your choices and maybe even share your values. It's like forming a guild in an MMO. You want teammates who've got your back and share your mission, not those who'll lead you into unnecessary PvP battles.

Remember dude, every level of life, especially your preteen years, is about figuring out who you are, and sometimes, that means standing out instead of blending in. It's cool to take the road less traveled. After all, the most epic quests often start with a choice that's different from everyone else's. Stay true to your path, level up in confidence, and keep your faith as your guide. Yes, it can be scary to stand out. But who knows? You might just inspire your crew to think differently, and suddenly, you're not just following the game—you're setting the pace.

And here's the thing: being confident in who you are and what you stand for is like having the best armor in the game. Actually, it's not about what you stand for, but WHO makes you stand. I'm talking about Jesus! Just like David, you can be sure He's got your back. And you know what? Jesus stood out like a sore thumb, so He totally gets how you feel. But He kept going because He knew it was totally worth it. He died on the cross for you, so you can be just as confident.

He's your map, your shield, your final quest, your ultimate treasure, and your recovery point. And I'm telling you, joining the crowd all the time so you don't stand out is not as safe or cool as you think. It's like knowing the best character in the game and following Him instead of trying to copy someone else's gameplay. Remember Jesus—He will make you stand.

Prayer

Dear Lord, when I feel pressured to follow the crowd, give me the strength to stand firm in my faith. Help me to make choices that honor You and enjoy you more, even when it's hard. Remind me that with Your guidance, I can stay true to who I am in You. Amen

Fun Fact:

Chameleons change colors to stand out and express themselves. Similarly, you can stand out by being true to your faith. Embrace your inner chameleon and let your true colors shine!

Game: Peer Pressure Scenarios

Objective:

Learn to handle peer pressure and stay strong in your faith through role-play.

1. **Prepare Scenario Cards:**

   Create cards with peer pressure situations, like skipping homework, gossiping, or cheating.

2. **Explain the Game:**

   Draw a scenario card, think about how to respond, then act it out. Discuss different ways to handle the situation.

3. **Play and Reflect:**

   Role-play the scenarios, ensuring everyone participates. Afterward, discuss what you learned and how to apply these strategies in real life.

Build Your Confidence Quest

Jot down what makes you unique—your interests, boundaries, and values. Keep these in mind when facing pressure. Like focusing on a game's quest objective, staying true to yourself helps you resist peer pressure.

Skill check

> How does knowing that Jesus has your back give you
> confidence to make choices that might be different from
> everyone else's? How can you use this confidence to
> inspire your friends to think differently too?

....

....

....

....

Save Your Game Plan

....

....

....

....

Chapter 10
Boss Fight: Handling Bullies the Christian Way

ROMANS 12:19-21 (NIV)

"Do not take revenge, my dear friends, but leave room for God's wrath, for it is written: 'It is mine to avenge; I will repay,' says the Lord. On the contrary: 'If your enemy is hungry, feed him; if he is thirsty, give him something to drink. In doing this, you will heap burning coals on his head.' Do not be overcome by evil, but overcome evil with good."

Imagine you're in the middle of an intense game session, totally zoned in, when someone steps in, messes up your play, and laughs it off. Feels pretty rotten, right? Now, picture this happening not just in the gaming world but in real life—like someone constantly poking fun at you, spreading rumors, or excluding you just for the kicks. That's bullying, and it's no joke. Bullies come in all shapes and sizes, and they can turn what should be cool spaces—like school or the skate park—into a battleground.

Now, let's talk hero tactics. Remember how Jesus dealt with people who were less than friendly? When folks threw insults or worse, he didn't zap them with lightning or call down fire. Nope. He showed kindness, flipped the script by offering forgiveness, and moved on. It's that classic 'turn the other cheek' move. But let's break it down because turning the other cheek doesn't mean you stand there and let someone go all World Wrestling on you. It means not escalating the fight, not throwing back the same junk they're hurling at you. It's like in gaming—sometimes, the best strategy to disarm the opponent is to not play their game. Instead of just not playing the game, Jesus changed it completely. It was way more epic. He died for them—for real! Those soldiers who hit and spat at Him, and the crowds that yelled for His death and humiliation. He died for them too, to save them. Can you believe it?

But here's the real twist: sometimes, the person doing the bullying is dealing with their own battles that we don't see. It doesn't make what they do right, but it's like finding out the villain in a game has a sad backstory. Jesus even died for those bullies, and He cares about them too. They might be lost, angry, and sad, just like we feel sometimes. 'That sounds crazy! Are you asking me to care about bullies?' I know, it seems unfair. But God does some wild and amazing things. Don't worry; bullies still have to pay the price for their actions, and the same Jesus who died for them will also judge them fairly. As it says in Romans 12:19, 'It is mine to avenge, I will repay'. It's like in a game where everyone eventually faces the final boss—justice will be served.

But what do you do when you're the one in the crosshairs? First off, standing strong doesn't mean suffering in silence. If you're being bullied, it's more than okay—it's important—to talk to someone. It could be a teacher, a coach, or your parents. Yeah, it might feel super awkward to start that chat. You might worry about making it worse, but think of it this way: you're pulling in reinforcements, not tattling. It's about fortifying your defenses, not launching an attack, and certainly not starting one.

And here's something you might not hear often—pray for the bully. Sounds wild, right? But here's the deal: praying for someone doesn't mean you're okay with what they're doing. It's about seeking peace, healing, and maybe even understanding. It's asking God to work in their life and yours, to change the game for everyone involved.

Dealing with bullies is tough; no cheat codes or easy hacks about it. Sometimes, you might actually need to confront the bully. But remember, you're not alone in this. You've got a squad, both on high and right here, rooting for you. Keep your head up, your heart strong, and lean on those around you when things get too heavy. After all, every hero needs a team, and you, my friend, are definitely one of the good guys. Keep battling the good fight, and let's make those game spaces and school places a little brighter for everyone.

Prayer

Dear Jesus, when I face bullies and those who seek to hurt me, help me to respond with love and patience. Give me the courage to stand up for myself and others with kindness and grace. Teach me to pray for those who hurt me, knowing that Your love can change hearts. Amen.

Game: Handling Bullies with Kindness

Objective:
Practice responding to bullies with kindness through role-playing.

Prepare Scenario Cards:

Write down bullying situations, such as:

Scenario 1: Name-Calling

"Someone calls you names. How do you respond with kindness and strength?"

Scenario 2: Physical Bullying

"A bully pushes you. How do you stay safe and respectful?"

Scenario 3: Exclusion

"You're excluded from activities. How do you handle it while staying true to your faith?"

1. **Play the Game:**

   Draw a scenario card, act it out, and discuss how to handle the situation in a Christ-like way.

2. **Reflect:**

   After role-playing, discuss what you learned and how to apply these strategies in real life.

Skill check

> Have you ever thought about praying for someone who's been mean to you? How could asking God to help them—and you—bring peace to a tough situation?

....

....

....

....

Save Your Game Plan

....

....

....

....

Chapter 11
Solo Missions: What to Do When You're Left Out

ROMANS 8:38-39 (NIV)

"For I am convinced that neither death nor life, neither angels nor demons, neither the present nor the future, nor any powers, neither height nor depth, nor anything else in all creation, will be able to separate us from the love of God that is in Christ Jesus our Lord."

Ever had that moment when you're the last one picked for a team, or worse, not picked at all? Or those times when everyone's got an invite to a party except you? Yeah, that stings like accidentally stepping on a LEGO brick—sharp and unexpected. It's like you're the only one without a teammate in a duo match, watching from the sidelines. Feeling left out can really mess with your head and heart, making you question your worth. But here's some real talk: those feelings of being on the outside? They don't define your true value, not even close.

So, what do you do when you find yourself sitting on the bench of life? First up, let's hit up the Good Book for some comfort. Ever read some of the Psalms? These are like the ancient tweets of people pouring out their hearts, and man, some of those are all about feeling lonely and left out. Like Psalm 25:16, which says, "Turn to me and be gracious to me, for I am lonely and afflicted." Even back then, people felt the way you do now, and they turned those feelings into prayers, talking to God about everything. These verses remind us that feeling left out has been part of the human experience for ages, and guess what? You're never alone in those feelings. God's got a listening ear for all the highs and lows. And not only does He listen to you, but He also comforts you. In Romans 8:38-39, He says that nothing can separate you from His love. Not even feeling left out!

But why does feeling left out hurt so much? Well, that's because when we're left out, we feel like we're not valued. We feel like we're tossed aside and not part of something awesome. And that can sting big time. That's why we need to let the truth of Romans 8:38 grow in our hearts. We need to remember that God loves us and feel loved, cherished, and valued. And it goes even further than that—there's no obstacle to the love God showed us in Jesus. No death, no time, no powers, NOTHING can stop it. It's like being perpetually hugged by a loving father who will never toss you away. Imagine being wrapped in an unbreakable, warm blanket of love that never lets you go. It's that epic.

Now, finding your squad where you feel you belong can be a game-changer. Maybe it's not the popular crowd at school but a group where you share real interests. It could be a church youth group where everyone's a bit of a misfit or a club where you geek out over robotics or fantasy football. The cool part? You don't have to be MVP to feel valued. It's all about being part of a team where everyone has something unique to contribute, just like in a relay race where every runner plays a part in crossing the finish line. And remember, you're already on the ultimate winning team—Team Jesus. He's the coach who's picked you first for His team, not for your skills or cool factor, but simply because you matter to Him, big time.

Sometimes, though, you might find yourself flying solo, and it feels like you're benched. That's when you can discover the hidden superpower of solitude. Spending time alone isn't about being lonely; it's about connecting with God on a one-on-one level. Like those quiet moments before a storm in a game when you're gearing up for the next big battle, use that solo time to gear up spiritually. Pray, meditate on Scripture, or just tell God about your day—the good, the bad, and the ugly. These moments can strengthen you, helping you wear that warm blanket of love again and again, kind of like leveling up in secret, so when you step back into the game, you're more equipped than ever.

Building your self-worth on this foundation is like constructing your base on bedrock in Minecraft—stable and secure. Know this: your value isn't about who includes you or who doesn't. It's about who you are in God's eyes. He's crafted you with all your quirks, talents, and dreams for a purpose. So even on days when you feel like an NPC in someone else's game, remember, in God's story, you're always the main character. Keep that head up, champion. The game's far from over, and with God, you're always set for a comeback, no matter how many times you feel left out. Keep those spirits high, your faith strong, and watch as God turns those solo quests into epic adventures.

Prayer

Dear God, sometimes I feel left out and alone, and it really hurts. Help me to remember that you are always with me and that you will never throw me away. Show me how to find comfort in Your presence and guide me to new friendships where I am valued and included. Amen.

Fun Fact: The Resilient Penguin

Penguins are incredibly resilient, facing harsh conditions by sticking together. If one is left out, it finds a way to rejoin or form a new group. If you ever feel left out, remember the penguin—find new friends or activities where you can belong. Like a penguin, you have the strength to keep going and find your place.

Game: Handling Exclusion with Kindness

Objective:
Learn how to handle feeling left out and include others.

Scenarios:

Not Invited to a Party: "You find out friends had a party without you. How do you respond?"

Left Out of a Game: "Kids won't let you join a game at recess. What do you do?"

Ignored in a Conversation: "Friends ignore you when you try to join a conversation. How do you handle it?"

1. **Play:**

   Draw a scenario, think it through, and act it out. Discuss positive ways to respond and include others.

2. **Reflect:**

   Discuss lessons learned and how to apply these strategies to make sure everyone feels included.

Skill check

> How can you remember that God loves you no matter what, even when others don't treat you well? What's one thing you can do to feel closer to God when you're feeling left out?

....

....

....

....

Save Your Game Plan

....

....

....

....

Chapter 12

Anxiety Boss Battle: Keeping Cool Under Pressure

MATTHEW 6:25-27 (NIV)

"Therefore I tell you, do not worry about your life, what you will eat or drink; or about your body, what you will wear. Is not life more than food, and the body more than clothes? Look at the birds of the air; they do not sow or reap or store away in barns, and yet your heavenly Father feeds them. Are you not much more valuable than they? Can any one of you by worrying add a single hour to your life?"

Ever felt like your stomach's in knots right before a big game or when a test paper's staring you down? That squirmy, butterfly-chasing feeling? Yep, that's anxiety, and believe it or not, it's a normal part of the human software package. Anxiety is like your brain's alarm system—it goes off when there's a potential threat. It's supposed to help you stay alert and ready. Think of it as your body's way of saying, "Heads up, we need to be on our toes for this one!" But sometimes, just like a glitchy alarm clock that goes off at 3 AM, anxiety gets a little too eager and rings the alarm too loud or too often. That's when it starts to mess with your game instead of helping you play better.

In the grand adventure of life, even heroes like us need some Biblical power-ups to manage those anxious jitters. Remember what Jesus said in Matthew 6? He told us not to worry about tomorrow because each day has enough trouble of its own. He's like the ultimate coach, reminding us to focus on how unbeatable God's high score is and how much He cares for you, not on the 'what ifs' of tomorrow. Whether it's that algebra test or the championship game, worrying won't add a single point to your score. Instead, Jesus points us to rely on God, the ultimate Game Master, who knows the game inside and out and cares about every player personally.

It says it right there in Matthew 6:26, 'Are you not much more valuable than they?' You are SUPER VALUABLE to Him. Way more valuable. And if you have something valuable, you totally take care of it. Just like how God's got your back, He will take care of what you need. He reminds us throughout the Bible—about 365 times—'Do not fear.' That's like getting a daily power-up against fear every single morning!

Now, let's talk tactics for keeping those nerves in check. First up, breathing exercises. Sounds simple, right? But you'd be surprised how a few deep breaths can reset your system faster than you can say "respawn." Next time you feel the anxiety levels ramping up, try this: breathe in slowly through your nose, hold it for a few seconds, then breathe out slowly through your mouth. Repeat a few times. It's like hitting the pause button, giving your body a chance to chill and catch up.

Next up, remember God's promises for you. Try memorizing some Bible verses like Matthew 6:25. It's like loading up your weapon with ammo. It helps your mind focus on how awesome God is and how much He loves you. When you feel anxious, recite these verses to remind yourself of His love and power. Another pro tip? Prayer. It's not just about asking for stuff; it's like opening a direct chat with God about what's bugging you. Tell Him what's on your mind. It's like offloading those heavy backpacks during a long hike.

Then, set a plan. Just because God says don't be anxious doesn't mean we don't need to work. It should actually push us to organize how to get things done, always expecting that God will come through and keep us going. And focusing on one day at a time? That's key. Instead of freaking out over the entire season, focus on winning one game at a time, one play at a time. Break down your worries into manageable checkpoints.

Navigating through the maze of school, friendships, and growing up can some-times feel like you're constantly dodging obstacles. Anxiety pops up, challenges loom large, and it can get overwhelming. But remember, just like in any good game, you've got tools and power-ups at your disposal. Use them. Breathe, Re-member, Pray, and Plan, and keep that anxiety list as a reminder of your wins. You're not in this game alone; you've got the best Coach rooting for you, and a whole team of fellow players (aka friends and family) cheering you on. So keep your head in the game, your heart steady, and your eyes on the prize. God's got the rest covered.

Prayer

Dear Lord, when anxiety takes hold and I feel overwhelmed, please fill my heart with Your peace. Remind me to trust in You and Your plan, knowing that You are always in control and care for me. Help me to stay calm and confident, relying on Your strength in every situation. Amen.

Fun Fact: The Calm of a Turtle

Did you know that turtles have a unique way of staying calm under pressure? When they sense danger, they retreat into their shells for protection and take a moment to assess the situation. This slow and steady approach helps them stay safe and collected. When you feel anxious or overwhelmed, try taking a cue from the turtle—find a quiet space, take a few deep breaths, and give yourself a moment to Remember, Pray and Plan. Remember, staying calm and taking things one step at a time can help you handle any pressure with grace and confidence.

Anxiety List Level-Up

Here's a cool trick to keep track of those pesky anxieties—create an 'Anxiety List.' Every time something makes you anxious, jot it down. Then, next to it, write down what happened after. Did it turn out as bad as you thought? Did you handle it okay? Over time, you'll see patterns and maybe realize those dragons aren't as big as they appear. Plus, you can track how often God comes through for you, which He does, because, well, He's pretty awesome like that.

***

Skill check

> Jesus says we're super valuable to God. How does knowing this help you worry less about things? What's one way you can remind yourself that God's got your back when you start to feel anxious?

....

....

....

....

Save Your Game Plan

....

....

....

....

Home Base

WELCOME TO THE HQ, the command center, the heart of operations—or, as most folks call it, home. Now, before you roll your eyes and think, "Oh great, another lecture about cleaning my room," hold up. This isn't about turning you into Mr. Clean or getting you to eat all your veggies (though, hey, those aren't bad ideas). It's about the cool, sometimes complicated, and definitely crucial stuff that happens at home, like figuring out how to deal with the 'rents, understanding why your family does things a certain way, and how to keep your cool when your little bro is being extra annoying. So, let's jump right in, and no, we're not starting with a chore list!

Chapter 13
Following the Leader: Why Obeying Parents Matters

Ephesians 6:1-3 (NIV)

"Children, obey your parents in the Lord, for this is right. 'Honor your father and mother'—which is the first commandment with a promise—'so that it may go well with you and that you may enjoy long life on the earth.'"

Let's face it: listening to your parents can sometimes feel like being in a never-ending tutorial level in a game where you just can't wait to start playing for real. But before you think about skipping the cutscenes, let's hit pause and check out why this stuff matters. Ever heard of the commandment, "Honor your father and mother"? Yeah, it's one of the Big Ten, right up there with "Do not steal" and "No lying." This isn't just old-school advice; it's a major life hack for smoother gameplay at home.

Now, obeying your parents isn't about them bossing you around just because they can. It's more like they're the experienced players who have been through the levels before and have some pro tips that could save you from falling into traps. Think of their rules as the game boundaries set to keep you from wandering into the enemy's territory or getting zapped. When they set a curfew or limit your screen time, it's not because they want to spoil your fun. It's more like they're saying, "Hey, we know there's quicksand around that area, let's steer clear," or "That level has some tough enemies, gear up before you head in."

And the deeper meaning behind those warnings is that they love you and want the best for you. It's like whining about wanting to jump in quicksand when we all know that's just plain dumb. Instead, they steer you towards jumping into a nice, refreshing pool, enjoying all its coolness with your friends. Just like that, your parents want to protect what's valuable and precious to them—you! They also want to help you make smart choices in life. To make sure that happens, there are rules set up, and they have to get you ready to face the big boss fight of growing up. Believe it or not, one day, you might need to face the fight without them, and you should be better equipped by then.

In fact, God is often called a loving father. His rules aren't meant to cramp your style but to treat you like His kids. I mean, even Jesus honored His mom and dad. It's true! When Jesus was a kid, He listened to Mary and Joseph and respected them. There's this cool story in the Bible where Jesus, even though He was super wise, went back home with His parents and obeyed them. And get this—when Jesus was on the cross, He made sure His mom would be taken care of by His friend John. That shows how much He loved and honored His mom.

Now, what's in it for you? Well, sticking to the rules can actually score you more freedom. Sounds weird, right? But here's the deal: when you show you're good at handling smaller quests, like doing homework without being reminded or keeping your room monster-free (yeah, that means tidy), you level up in their eyes. They start trusting you with bigger quests, like hanging out later with friends or managing more of your own gaming time. It's all about building that trust stat in your family character sheet.

But what if the rules seem way out of line, like they're stuck in the past century? Here's a pro move: communicate. Instead of going rogue and ignoring the rules, try talking it out. Explain your side of the story, listen to theirs, and maybe you'll find a middle ground. Like, maybe agree to check in with a text if you're out late, so they don't stay up worrying you've been abducted by aliens. And if talking it out feels like trying to beat a final boss with low HP, take a moment to pray about it. Ask God to help you understand each other and to give you the patience and wisdom to deal with family rules like a champ.

Don't forget, this isn't a solo mission. You've got teammates—your family—who are all playing this game together with you. By understanding the rules, respecting each other's roles, and communicating like the champions you are, you'll not only level up individually but also boost your family team stats. And who knows? With enough practice, you might just find that home base can be one of the coolest levels in the game of life.

Prayer

Dear God, thank You for my parents and the guidance they provide. Help me to understand that obeying them is not just about following rules, but about honoring and respecting the love and wisdom they offer. Teach me to listen with an open heart and to appreciate their care as a reflection of Your love for me. Amen.

Reflect and React Challenge

Write down tough home rules and why they exist. Understanding your parents' perspective can help you propose a fair plan for more freedom. *Example:* Curfew at 9 PM—parents worry about your safety.

Game: Strengthening Family Bonds

1. **Role Reversal:** Act as the parent to understand their perspective.
   Example: Explain why bedtime is important for a child's health.

2. **Chore Challenge:** Complete a chore to show responsibility.
   Example: Sweep the kitchen floor thoroughly and carefully.

3. **Communication Skills:** Practice respectful conversation to build trust.
   Example: Discuss why you want to attend a friend's party and listen to your parents' concerns.

4. **Gratitude:** Write a thank-you note to strengthen your bond.
   Example: Thank your parents for helping with a school project.

5. **Rule Reflection:** Discuss the purpose of a home rule to understand its value.
   Example: Talk about why limited screen time helps with focus and sleep.

***

Skill check

> How is obeying your parents like following the rules in a game, and why do you think God wants you to do it?

....

....

....

....

Save Your Game Plan

....

....

....

....

Chapter 14

Home Base Changes: Coping with Divorce and Separation

PSALM 46:1-2 (NIV)

"God is our refuge and strength, an ever-present help in trouble. Therefore we will not fear, though the earth give way and the mountains fall into the heart of the sea."

So, let's chat about something a bit heavy—divorce and separation. For some of you, this might hit close to home, or maybe you've seen a friend go through it. It's like having your life map suddenly torn up and redrawn without any warning. Everything feels different, and not in a cool, adventurous way. It can feel more like trying to play your favorite multiplayer game, but the server keeps glitching. But here's something to remember: even though home life is changing, the game isn't over, not by a long shot.

First off, it's totally normal to feel like a tornado just blasted through your life. You might feel sad, confused, or even angry. That's okay. It's part of the deal. Think of King David in the Bible. When he was having a tough time, he didn't bottle it up; he poured all his feelings out, just like in Psalm 46:1-2. He was real about the mess, no filters. And that's something you can do too. Whether it's through writing, making art, or even pounding out some beats on your drum set, expressing what you're feeling is like hitting the release valve on a pressure cooker—it helps keep things from boiling over.

Hanging onto your faith might feel like trying to hold onto a greased pig some-times, especially when everything feels upside down. But here's the thing: those stories in the Bible about God being our rock aren't just nice sayings for throw pillows. They're the real deal. Like, when Jesus said He'd be with us always, He meant it. No "only on sunny days" clause. Staying connected with youth group, church, or just chatting with God can be like finding an oasis in the middle of a desert. It's where you get to recharge, find strength, and remember that even though the ground is shaking, you're not standing on it alone.

Now, about your parents. They're not perfect, and things can definitely get complicated and messy. You might not get it at all. And it's totally not your fault. I get it—you might wish everything could go back to how it was. Maybe it will, but maybe it won't. Family dinners might look different, or you might have two homes now. It's like when a game updates: the interface might change, but the mission stays the same. The mission here? Making sure you know you're loved, no matter what level you're playing on. Do you know who the perfect parent is? Jesus. The whole Earth might be shaking, but imagine Him gripping your hand, never letting go. In His hand, you are safe, you are valuable, you are strong.

Reaching out for help can feel like admitting you're the noob in a lobby of pros, but everyone needs a squad to back them up. Talking to someone who gets it, like a pastor, counselor, or teacher, can be a game-changer. They can help you navigate the new maps you're finding yourself in, equip you with the right gear (aka coping strategies), and remind you that every hero needs a hand sometimes. Plus, they can be a safe place to unload when the boss battles—aka emotions—get intense.

Remember, change is part of every epic story. It's the plot twists that make the narrative rich and the victories sweet. Through all the ups and downs, the reboots, and the new beginnings, you've got a team in your corner—both at home and up above, cheering you on every step of the way. So keep your head up, your heart open, and your game on point. You've got this, and God's got you.

Prayer

Dear God, when my home goes through big changes like divorce or separation, it can be really tough and confusing. Please give me comfort and strength to cope with these changes and help me to trust in Your love and presence through it all. Surround my family with Your peace and guide us to support and understand each other during this difficult time. Amen.

Activity: "My Feelings Journal"

Objective:
Create a journal to express and understand your feelings about changes at home.

1. **Introduce the Journal:**
   Create a "Feelings Journal" to write or draw your thoughts and emotions.

2. **Personalize:**
   Decorate your journal with your name, drawings, and stickers to make it uniquely yours.

3. **Guided Prompts:**
   Start with these prompts:

   - "Today I feel..."

   - "I feel sad when..."

   - "A change I'm worried about is..."

   - "One thing I wish would change is..."

4. **Use the Journal:**
   Write or draw in your journal whenever you need to. It's your space to express yourself.

Closing:
Your journal is a safe space to sort through your emotions whenever you need it.

Skill check

> When life feels like it's falling apart, like during a big
> change at home, how can you remember that God is
> your safe place and strength? What's one way you can
> lean on Him and find help, even when things get tough?

....

....

....

....

Save Your Game Plan

....

....

....

....

Chapter 15

Teammate or Rival? Turning Sibling Battles into Friendships

Genesis 50:20-21 (NIV):

"You intended to harm me, but God intended it for good to accomplish what is now being done, the saving of many lives. So then, don't be afraid. I will provide for you and your children." And he reassured them and spoke kindly to them.

Ever felt like your home is an arena where you and your siblings are constantly competing? Whether it's for the last slice of pizza or who gets control of the TV remote, it seems like there's always something to argue about. But guess what? Sibling rivalry is as old as, well, siblings! Take Joseph and his brothers from the Bible (Genesis 50:20), for example. They threw him into a pit and sold him off to traders because they were jealous of the special coat his dad gave him (talk about extreme sibling rivalry, right?). But here's the twist—this story goes from rivalry to epic forgiveness and family unity. You see, God can take even the worst situations and turn them into something good. Totally epic!

So, why do these homegrown feuds happen? Often, it's about competition for attention or resources, just like two characters in a game vying for the same power-up. Sometimes, it's about differences in personalities and interests. Think of it this way: if you're a quiet gamer who likes strategy puzzles, and your sibling is all about high-energy action games, clashes might seem inevitable. But here's a cool thing—these differences can actually be your strength if you learn to appreciate them.

Now, let's talk about leveling up your sibling game. One mega strategy is spending quality time together. Not just sitting in the same room scrolling through your phones, but actually doing stuff together. Maybe you both dig movies—why not have a weekly movie night where you take turns picking the film? Or if you're into gaming, find a co-op game that needs teamwork. This isn't just about having fun; it's about building a team dynamic where you have each other's backs.

Communication is your power-up in turning sibling rivalry into camaraderie. And no, this doesn't mean shouting louder to be heard; it's about learning how to express what you're feeling without turning it into World War III. Start using "I" statements like, "I feel ignored when you talk over me," instead of "You never listen!" See the difference? It's like choosing dialogue options in a game that leads to better alliances rather than turning everyone into an enemy. Active listening is another key skill. This means really hearing what your sibling is saying, not just planning your counterattack while they speak. It's like pausing your game to really focus on an important cutscene—you give it your full attention.

Forgiveness might sound like a legendary skill reserved for saints and superheroes, but it's actually something anyone can learn. Holding grudges is like carrying a heavy backpack during a marathon—it slows you down and makes everything more exhausting. Letting go of that weight frees you up to enjoy the race. When Joseph forgave his brothers, it wasn't because what they did was okay. He forgave them because he saw that God used those events to save his people and teach him humility. Forgiveness in your sibling saga can be a game-changer. It transforms your home life from a battleground to a team base.

Next time things get heated, think of Joseph's comeback. Try flipping the script from competition to teamwork—whether it's bonding over cool hobbies, keeping it real with open chats, or hitting the reset button with some forgiveness. These aren't just ways to chill at home—they're skills that can turn your sibling from rival to BFF. Who knows? Your bro or sis might end up being your top ally. So, keep the convo flowing, squad up, and always be ready to forgive. Your family could become the ultimate dream team.

Prayer

Dear God, sometimes it feels hard to get along with my siblings, and we end up as rivals instead of friends. Help us to see the good in each other and to grow in patience and understanding. Teach us to support one another, turning our rivalry into a strong and loving friendship. Amen.

Cool fact

Even Jesus had siblings, and He showed us how to turn rivalry into friendship. When Jesus' siblings didn't believe in Him at first, He still treated them with love and patience. Over time, they became some of His closest followers. So next time you and your sibling are at each other's throats, remember that with a little love and understanding, you can go from being foes to being best friends. Jesus showed us that it's possible!

Skill check

> When you and your siblings clash, how can you remember Joseph's story and choose to turn the rivalry into teamwork? What's one way you can start seeing your sibling as a teammate instead of a rival?

....

....

....

....

Save Your Game Plan

....

....

....

....

Chapter 16
Disconnected at Home: When Your Family Doesn't Get Your Faith

John 15:18-19 (NIV)

"If the world hates you, keep in mind that it hated me first. If you belonged to the world, it would love you as its own. As it is, you do not belong to the world, but I have chosen you out of the world. That is why the world hates you"

So, you've got this fire inside you, a spark lit by your faith, and you're all set to share that light, right? But what if the fam just doesn't get it? Maybe they're not into the whole church scene, or they have different beliefs, or maybe talking about faith feels like trying to explain why pineapple on pizza is actually a brilliant idea—it just leads to raised eyebrows or eye rolls. But here's the thing, sharing your faith at home doesn't have to be like dropping a controversial new game patch everyone's skeptical about. It's more about showing them the game is worth playing through your actions and gentle words.

First up, expressing your faith gently is key. It's like introducing someone to a new game. You wouldn't start by telling them every single rule and strategy. That's overwhelming! Instead, you'd show them the cool features, let them see why you love playing it, and give them space to get intrigued. Sharing your faith can be similar. It's not about bombarding your family with verses or theological debates. It's more about letting them see what faith does in your life. How does it make you a better brother and a kinder person, or how does it give you peace during the boss battles of life? Think about how God dealt with Israel, which is often described as a father-and-son relationship. Despite their constant wandering off, He kept showing up, guiding and loving, instead of just breaking the relationship. Or take the prodigal son's dad—didn't force the son to stay home, right? But his love was undeniable when the son returned.

Finding common ground can strengthen your cred like nothing else. Maybe your family loves to spend time outdoors. You could share how you feel God's presence in nature and how it's like a big, beautiful level designed by a top-notch Developer. Or perhaps during family movie night, talk about the themes in the movie that resonate with your faith—things like redemption, courage, or sacrifice. It's not about making every conversation a Sunday school lesson, but about weaving your perspective into everyday life in a way that's natural and relatable. Continue showing love and respect, keeping those family bonds tight. Remember, your actions often speak louder than a sermon, showing the real-life power-up you get from your faith.

Patience and prayer aren't just good power-ups for your faith—they're essential tactics in your gameplay, especially when it comes to bridging gaps in understanding. Think of them as your long-term strategy buffs. Praying for your family not only changes things for them, but it keeps your heart in the right place too. It's like keeping your gear oiled and ready—it helps you stay focused, patient, and loving, even when the immediate results aren't visible. And patience? Well, it's that epic skill that every seasoned gamer needs. It means understanding that everyone plays at their own pace. Just as some might take longer to learn a game, others might take time to understand or embrace your faith. Keep the chat lines open, keep your cool, and let your consistent love and commitment do the talking.

But why can't they see how awesome God is? Did I mess up? I don't want them to hate me." I get it, it's tough. Being tight with family is a big deal—they're the ones who've been through everything with you. And guess what? It's not just kids who deal with this; a lot of adults face it too, with their parents, kids, siblings, aunts, and uncles. Even Jesus was misunderstood and rejected by His own family and hometown. In John 15:18- 19, Jesus even gives us a heads-up that people might not always get it, and sometimes that includes our families.

But here's the deal: our awesome God will never bail on you. He's chosen you, and you'll always have a place with Him. Trust me, being with Him is way better. Plus, no problem is too big for Him, even changing your family's hearts.

Sometimes, it just feels easier to give up and play solo. But hang in there. Keep sharing your faith through love, find that common ground where you can connect, and keep leveling up your patience and prayer stats. The impact might not always be immediate, but over time, you might just find your family more open and curious about why your faith makes you so stoked. And who knows? They might even join you at the next level, ready to explore this great adventure alongside you.

Prayer

Dear Lord, sometimes my family doesn't understand my faith, and it can feel lonely and challenging. Please give me the strength to stay true to my beliefs and the patience to love them despite our differences. Help me to share my faith with kindness and grace, trusting that You will work in their hearts. Amen.

***

Activity: Write a Letter

Write a letter to a family member about your faith. You don't have to give it to them if you don't want to. This is just for you to practice expressing your thoughts and feelings.

Use these prompts to help you get started:

"Dear [Family Member], I want to share something important to me..."

"My faith means..."

"I believe in..."

"My favorite part of my faith is..."

"A time when my faith helped me was..."

"I hope you can understand that..."

Skill check

> When your family or friends don't understand your faith, how can you stay strong like Jesus did? What's one way you can show them God's love without pushing too hard?

....

....

....

....

Save Your Game Plan

....

....

....

....

School Survival Guide

ALRIGHT, BUCKLE UP, BECAUSE we're diving headfirst into the wild, sometimes whacky world of school. Think of it as the ultimate multiplayer arena where you're juggling quests like homework, tests, and that epic boss battle known as making friends. Plus, there's the side quests like not tripping in the hallway or trying to dodge cafeteria food that looks sus, like it's from another planet. School's got its challenges, but with the right strategies, you can totally level up your school experience from "meh" to "awesome"!

Chapter 17
Balancing the Grind: Homework vs. Hobbies

PROVERBS 6:6-8 (NIV)

"Go to the ant, you sluggard; consider its ways and be wise! It has no commander, no overseer or ruler, yet it stores its provisions in summer and gathers its food at harvest."

1 Corinthians 10:31 (NIV)

"So whether you eat or drink or whatever you do, do it all for the glory of God."

Let's talk real talk: balancing homework and your hobbies can sometimes feel like trying to fit your entire collection of action figures on one tiny shelf. It's about making everything fit without having Spider-Man's foot jabbing into Batman's face. Prioritizing your time is kinda like being a master planner in your favorite strategy game. You gotta know what mission to tackle first, what can wait, and how to make sure you're not burning out faster than a cheap firework.

First step? Planning. We humans, just like our ant friends in Proverbs 6:8, can actually plan ahead. We can look at our week and decide when we're going to study for that beast of a math test and when we can chill out and game. It's about making a schedule that isn't just doable, but also leaves room for fun. Because all work and no play makes Jack a super bored boy, right? Here's the kicker though – sometimes, you've gotta make sacrifices. Maybe that means playing one less hour of video games on a school night to prep for that big science project. It's tough, but think of it as investing time now for epic wins later.

Setting realistic goals is super important too. Let's be honest, not every class is going to be your jam. You might be a wizard in history but feel like you're trying to decode alien technology in math. And that's okay! Setting goals like improving a grade bit by bit or spending extra time on tough subjects can help big time. It's not about being perfect; it's about pushing yourself to be better bit by bit. And hey, when you reach those goals? Celebrate! Treated yourself to an extra episode of your favorite show or some extra gaming time. You earned it!

Now, how about mixing a little faith into both schoolwork and hobbies? Whether you're sketching like a pro for art class or scoring the winning goal at soccer practice, you can do it all for God's glory. It might sound kinda wild, but think about it. Every quiz you ace and every game you win is like a way to say thanks to the Big Guy upstairs for giving you the skills and brains to rock it. It makes even the boring stuff feel special, knowing you're relying on God in everything you do. So, whether you're doing homework, playing sports, or just chilling with friends, remember you're playing for God's team. Enjoy everything, do your best, and know that He's cheering you on every step of the way.

Balancing school and play doesn't have to be a dreaded grind. With a bit of planning, realistic goal-setting, and the right mix of work and fun, you can make your school days feel a little less like a chore and a lot more like a well-played game. And remember, with each day, you're not just getting through your to-do list; you're setting up for bigger wins in the game of life where the achievements feel just as great as leveling up in your favorite video game. So, gear up, plan well, and let's ace this level together!

Prayer

Dear Lord, thank You for the interests and talents You've given me. Help me to balance my homework and hobbies wisely, so I can succeed in my studies while also enjoying the activities I love. Grant me the discipline and time management skills I need to honor You in all I do. Amen.

***

Activity: "Balancing Act: Homework and Hobbies"

1. **List Activities:**

   On paper, create two columns: "Homework" and "Hobbies." List your school tasks under "Homework" and your favorite activities under "Hobbies."

2. **Estimate Time:**

   Estimate how long each homework task and hobby will take.

3. **Create a Schedule:**

   Make a weekly schedule. Block out time for school and homework first, then add your hobbies. Include breaks, and use different colors to highlight each.

4. **Prioritize:**

   Use sticky notes to mark the most important homework tasks and hobbies. Consider due dates and what matters most to you.

5. **Manage Time:**

   Set a timer for homework sessions, then take a break for hobbies. Avoid distractions by working in a quiet place, and combine homework with hobbies when possible.

Skill check

> How can planning your time, like the ant in Proverbs, help you balance school and fun? What's one way you can do your best in everything, even the stuff you don't like, to honor God?

....

....

....

Save Your Game Plan

....

....

....

....

Chapter 18
Shining at School: Sharing Faith Like a Pro

1 Peter 3:15 (NIV)

"But in your hearts revere Christ as Lord. Always be prepared to give an answer to everyone who asks you to give the reason for the hope that you have. But do this with gentleness and respect."

So, you're rocking your faith like a stealthy ninja, low-key and cool, but what about when you're in the wild jungles of school? It's like stepping into a brightly-lit arena where everyone can see your moves. Showing your faith here isn't about pulling out a megaphone and shouting verses during lunch break. Nope, it's more like being that one gamer who's known for being fair, chill, and seriously good at teaming up. It's about living out your faith through your actions, decisions, and the way you treat others, kinda like wearing a team jersey that shows whose side you're on without needing to say a word.

Talking about faith at school can feel like a tricky game. You gotta know the rules and play smart. Sharing your faith is like knowing when to make a move in a strategy game and when to chill. It's about finding the right moment to talk about your faith in a cool and kind way, not like a bull in a china shop. Some friends will be curious, and others might not want to chat about beliefs. And that's totally okay. The key is to share your faith sincerely and gently, and remember, it's God who changes hearts, not you. So relax, be a good friend, and who knows, they might want to know more about your amazing God.

But let's be real; not everyone is going to cheer you on. Some might throw shade or challenge what you believe. That's when you need to gear up for some spiritual defense. Handling opposition with grace is like dodging in a dodgeball game – you gotta see it coming and know how to move. Stay calm, keep your cool, and use those moments to show what faith under pressure looks like. True strength isn't about how loudly you can argue, but how calmly and kindly you can stand your ground. And when things get tough, remember, the ultimate God not only warns you that it's normal to face shade for what you believe, but He also reassures your heart that you are valued and loved, even if it means disagreeing with others.

They say you're dumb or call you names – not true. They say you're hateful – NOPE. They avoid you or laugh at you – not gonna work. Like David, you can confidently say Psalm 31:13-14 (NIV):

"For I hear many whispering, 'Terror on every side!' They conspire against me and plot to take my life. But I trust in you, Lord; I say, 'You are my God.'

Turn to verses like this that remind you about God and His awesomeness, and let Him be your strength when the game gets intense. God's got your back, like the best teammate ever, so trust Him to help you navigate through the tough stuff.

Living out your faith at school is all about walking the talk. It's showing up every day as a representative of your faith, ready to be kind, fair, and genuine, no matter what level or boss battle the school day throws at you. It's about making your faith as much a part of your school life as homework and hangouts. And who knows? Your way of playing the game might just inspire someone else to join your team. So keep your head up, your heart strong, and your game on point. Let's light up your school like a well-played level in the greatest adventure ever!

***

Prayer

Dear God, thank You for the opportunity to share my faith at school. Help me to be a light, showing Your love and kindness to everyone I meet. Give me the courage to speak about You and the wisdom to know the right words to say, so that others can see Your goodness through me. Amen.

***

Activity time

Faith Story

Task: Share a short story about a time when your faith helped you or someone else. Write it down and discuss it with the group.

Message: Sharing personal experiences can inspire others and show the impact of faith in everyday life.

Random Acts of Kindness

Task: List three acts of kindness you can do at school to show God's love. Share your ideas with the group.

Message: Showing kindness is a practical way to demonstrate your faith and be a light to others.

Encouraging Words

Task: Write down three encouraging phrases or Bible verses you can share with classmates who might need a boost.

Message: Offering words of encouragement can make a big difference and reflect your faith

***

Skill check

> How can you show your faith at school without being pushy, like a good teammate who helps others? What's one way you can be ready to share why you believe in God, while still being kind and respectful?

....

....

....

....

Save Your Game Plan

....

....

....

....

Chapter 19

Science and Scripture: Co-Op Partners, Not Enemies

ROMANS 1:20 (NIV)

"For since the creation of the world God's invisible qualities—his eternal power and divine nature—have been clearly seen, being understood from what has been made, so that people are without excuse."

Ever felt like you had to pick a side between being a science geek and a faith follower? Like they're two opposing teams in the ultimate league championship? Well, here's some game-changing info: science and faith are actually more like teammates than rivals. Seriously, they can totally high-five each other! Let's bust the myth that you gotta choose between your telescope and your Bible. Instead, think of them as different tools in your adventure kit, helping you explore and understand this wild world we're living in.

Paul had it right in Romans 1:20 when he said that we can catch glimpses of God's epic creativity just by checking out nature—the mountains, oceans, and even the weirdly awesome platypus. People instinctively know that the world is created with rules and beauty. It's like each scientific discovery peels back a layer of the universe's game design, showing us more of the Developer's master plan. So, when you're geeking out over the latest space pics from NASA or figuring out how to code your own game, you're actually uncovering parts of God's handiwork. Mind blown, right? Science isn't just about equations and experiments; it's a way to worship God by celebrating His incredible creation.

Now, let's squad up with some of history's MVPs in the faith and science league. Ever heard of a guy named Isaac Newton? Not only did this dude define the laws of motion and gravity, but he also spent a ton of time writing about biblical prophecy. And he's not riding solo.

There's Georges Lemaître, a priest who was the first to come up with what we now call the Big Bang theory. These guys didn't see science and faith as a PvP battle; they saw them as co-op partners working together to crack the universe's code. So next time someone tries to tell you that believing in God means you can't dig science, just drop a knowledge bomb about these faith-filled scientists who shaped our understanding of the cosmos.

Now, embracing both science and Scripture also means leveling up your critical thinking skills. It's like being in a complex game where you need to strategize and make decisions based on the best info available. When you come across a tricky topic like the creation vs. evolution debate, don't just camp on one side of the map. Explore both territories. What does the scientific evidence say? What does Scripture say? How can these perspectives complement each other instead of clashing? Remember, the Bible isn't a science textbook—it's more about the 'who' and 'why' of creation, not the 'how' and 'when.' So, keeping that in mind can help you navigate through tough discussions without losing your cool or your faith. And if you need help, don't be shy to ask your parents or the pastor at church. They'll be stoked to help you out!

Navigating the crossroads of science and faith doesn't have to feel like a solo quest in a dark forest. Think of it more as an epic team-up, where each discovery, whether from a lab or a parable, brings you closer to understanding the grand story God has written for us. So keep your curiosity fired up, your mind open, and your heart grounded in faith. Who knows? You might just find that science and Scripture together give you a more complete map of this adventure called life.

Prayer

Dear God, thank You for the wonders of science and the wisdom of Scripture. Help me to see how both reveal Your truth and greatness, working together to deepen my understanding of the world and my faith. Guide me to appreciate the harmony between science and Your Word, knowing that all truth comes from You. Amen.

Explore and Engage Exercise

Got a science project coming up? Here's a cool idea: choose a topic that mixes the awesome stuff in nature with what the Bible says. You could look at how taking care of the Earth matches what the Bible teaches about protecting the planet, or check out how amazing the human brain is and talk about how it shows God's creativity. Share what you find with your class or science club. It's a fun way to show how your faith makes you love science even more and gets everyone thinking and talking.

Skill check

> How can exploring science help you see more of God's awesome power and creativity? What's one way you can use both your faith and curiosity to understand the world around you better?

....

....

....

....

Save Your Game Plan

....

....

....

....

Chapter 20

Respawn After Failure: Dealing with Grades and Setbacks

PSALM 37:23-24 (NIV)

"The Lord makes firm the steps of the one who delights in him; though he may stumble, he will not fall, for the Lord upholds him with his hand."

Ever had one of those days where no matter how hard you try, you end up feeling like you're playing a game on expert mode with the difficulty cranked way up? Maybe you studied hard for a test and still didn't ace it, or you gave your all in tryouts but didn't make the team. It feels like a mega punch in the gut, right? Well, here's the scoop on handling those not-so-awesome moments without letting them turn your game—aka life—upside down.

First things first, dealing with academic setbacks like a bad grade isn't about shrugging it off with a "better luck next time" attitude. It's about turning that setback into a setup for a comeback. Every mistake you make, every challenge you face, is like a hidden level in a game, packed with lessons just waiting to be unlocked. So, you got a C instead of an A? Crack open that test and see where things went sideways. Was it the algebra problems? The essay question? Identifying your weak spots is like spotting the booby traps in a game—you know what to dodge next time.

But here's the kicker: it's not just about boosting your grades; it's about growing tougher, smarter, and more resilient. Think of it like leveling up in real life. Each challenge is a chance to increase your stats in perseverance and problem-solving.

And remember, the most epic heroes in games and stories aren't the ones who had an easy ride—they're the ones who faced tough stuff and came out stronger. The same goes for you. Every setback is a step up to something better, if you're willing to learn and push forward.

Now, let's flip the script and see what the Bible says about success and failure. It's clear that our worth isn't about our achievements or the trophies on our shelves. Nope, it's way deeper. It's about who we are in Christ. Think about it: God doesn't love you because you're the valedictorian or the MVP on your soccer team. He loves you because you're His—flaws, fumbles, and all. And that's freeing! If you're amazed by who God is and His love for you, Psalm 37:24 promises that God will hold you up with His hand. He won't let you stay down forever.

But what if I really tried my best? I put in a lot of effort. Should I give up? NO WAY. Sometimes, life can feel super unfair, even when you've given it your all. It's not about how hard you try; sometimes, that's just how things go in this messed-up world. But remember, God is always fair. We might not see it right now, but justice will come, and he will fix this messed-up world. And you might find that this is a chance to lean on God and enjoy His support. He'll help you through unfair times. And that's totally awesome.

Feeling like you're not good at anything special? Hold up, let's park there for a sec. Every single one of us has something unique to bring to the table, something that God has wired into us to shine in our own unique way. The Bible talks about different kinds of gifts, but it's the same God working in all of them (1 Corinthians 12:4-7). Your thing might not be math or football. Maybe it's making people laugh, creating killer art, or figuring out how to fix just about anything. Those aren't just random skills; they're gifts from God, ways you can make your mark on the world in your own awesome way.

And don't go solo. Seeking support from teachers, mentors, or school counselors isn't a sign of weakness; it's a smart strategy. These folks are like the guides in a game, the ones who have the maps and the tips that can help you navigate through tricky territories. They can offer new strategies, a little extra help, or just a listening ear when you need to unload.

Dealing with disappointments is part of life. How you handle them—whether you see them as roadblocks or stepping stones—can make all the difference. Remember, in Christ, you've got an unshakeable source of worth and strength. With Him, every setback is just the start of a comeback. So gear up, press play, and get ready to turn those letdowns into level-ups. Keep pushing, keep praying, and keep aiming for those epic wins, knowing that the ultimate victory has already been won for you.

Prayer

Dear Lord, sometimes I face disappointments, like getting grades that are lower than I hoped for. Please help me trust Your plan for my life and learn from these experiences. Give me the strength to keep trying my best and the wisdom to see the bigger picture beyond my disappointments. Amen.

***

Emotional Armor Up!

Building emotional resilience is like crafting armor in a forge. It takes heat, time, and a lot of hammering. But once it's done, it's invaluable. When disappointment hits, and it will, having that resilience means you can take the hit and keep moving. How do you build it? Start with Scripture. Verses like Philippians 4:13 remind us that we can do all things through Christ who strengthens us, and they aren't just nice sayings—they're power boosts for our souls. Pray for strength, talk about what's bugging you with people who care, and keep a journal of the tough times and how you got through them. Seeing your own track record of overcoming can be a huge boost when the going gets tough.

Skill check

> When life feels like you're stuck in a tough level, how can you remember that God's got your back and won't let you fall? What's one way you can turn a setback into a comeback, knowing God is helping you every step of the way?

....

....

....

....

Save Your Game Plan

....

....

....

....

Chapter 21

XP Goals: Setting Godly Goals for School Success

Isaiah 43:7

'Everyone who is called by my name, whom i created for my glory, whom i formed and made.'

Okay, let's talk about setting goals that are not just about acing your tests or smashing your high scores in games. We're diving into something deeper—godly goals. Now, you might be wondering, "What on Earth is a godly goal?" Well, it's kind of like setting up objectives in a game, but these goals align with what God wants for us. It's about aiming to glorify Him and enjoy Him in everything we do. Think of it this way: God's ultimate win was sending Jesus to save us. That's the level of dedication we're talking about—committing to goals that reflect His love and goodness through our everyday actions.

Setting goals that honor God starts with understanding what's really important. It's not just about getting straight A's or being the team captain. It's about growing in character, deepening your faith, and spreading kindness like that one super contagious yawn in class. These goals might include reading your Bible, praying, helping out more at home without being asked, or even sharing your faith with a friend who's curious. These aren't just nice things; they're steps that bring you closer to living a life that lights up for God.

Now, let's get smart—not just the 'acing your exams' kind of smart, but SMART goals smart. SMART stands for Specific, Measurable, Achievable, Relevant, and

Time-bound. It's a killer strategy to make sure your goals aren't just wishes but plans that you can actually pull off. Let's say you want to be more helpful at home. A SMART goal would look like this: "I will help with washing the dishes three times a week after dinner for the next month." See how specific and clear that is? You know exactly what to do, how often to do it, and for how long. Plus, it's totally doable and directly ties into being more responsible, which is definitely a godly trait.

And here's where it gets really powerful—prayer. When you're setting your goals, bring them before God in prayer. It's like talking game strategy with the Coach before you hit the field. This chat with God helps you match your plans with His, especially if you know how awesome God is from the Bible. It makes sure your goals are good for you and others too. It's like getting a thumbs-up from God saying, "Yeah, you're on the right track, buddy." Plus, praying about your goals gives you strength and persistence because, let's be real, sticking to goals can be tough, and having God in your corner is the ultimate power-up.

Achieving your goals is awesome, but celebrating them? Even better! And when you do, it's all about giving props to God because, without Him, none of it would be possible. Whether it's acing a test you studied hard for, or managing not to snap back when your little sis is being annoying again, take a moment to thank God for helping you nail it. Then, share that joy. Maybe tell your friends or your youth group what God helped you accomplish. It's like sparking a little more light in your corner of the world.

Celebrating isn't just about throwing a party. It's about recognizing how far you've come and how God's been part of every step. It builds your gratitude and strengthens your faith, showing you time and again how God turns your hard work and dedication into epic wins. Plus, it encourages others to chase after their own godly goals, creating a vibe of motivation and positivity that can totally transform your crew.

Ready to set some epic godly goals? Remember, make them SMART, soak them in prayer, celebrate your victories, and always, always give the glory up to God. Keep aiming high, knowing that the best rewards are the ones that last way beyond any school year—rewards that echo into eternity.

Prayer

Dear God, as I strive for success in school, help me to set goals that honor You. Guide me to work diligently and use my talents wisely, always seeking to glorify You in my efforts. Remind me that true success comes from following Your path and trusting in Your plans for my life. Amen.

***

Goal setting activity

Activity 1: Define Your Goals

Task: Write down three academic goals you want to achieve this school year. Think about how these goals honor God.

Activity 2: Plan Your Steps

Task: For each goal, write down the steps you need to take to achieve it. Be specific about what you will do.

Activity 3: Accountability Partner

Task: Pair up with a partner and share your goals. Discuss how you can support each other in achieving these goals.

Activity 4: Daily Prayer

Task: Write a short prayer asking God for help and guidance in achieving your school goals. Pray together as a group.

Activity 5: Overcoming Obstacles

Task: Think of potential obstacles that might get in the way of achieving your goals. Write down strategies to overcome these obstacles.

Activity 6: Celebrate Progress

Task: Set small milestones for each goal and decide on a reward for when you reach them. Share your milestones and rewards with the group.

***

Skill check

> What do you think is the biggest goal of your life—something that's even more important than getting good grades or winning at your favorite game?

....

....

....

....

Save Your Game Plan

....

....

....

....

Make a Difference with Your Review

"WHOEVER BRINGS BLESSING WILL be enriched, and one who waters will himself be watered." - Proverbs 11:25

Hey, awesome dude! Sharing God's word is like sharing a superpower—it spreads joy and blessings all around. By showing love and helping others find God's wisdom, you're making the world a better place!

Our mission? To make God's word easy to understand and fun to explore. If you've enjoyed the Totally Awesome Devotional, I'd love to hear what you think! Ask a parent to help you scan the QR code below and leave an honest review:

[Insert QR Code]

If you're all about helping others, then you're definitely our kind of person. I'm super pumped to see you grow spiritually through the upcoming Bible lessons.

Big thanks from the bottom of my heart. May God bless you big time. Let's give all the glory to Him!

Digital Discipleship

WELCOME TO THE DIGITAL jungle, my friends! It's like stepping into a new level with hidden traps and epic treasure chests. In this techno-savvy world, it's not just about mastering the latest game or becoming a social media star; it's about navigating this space like a true follower of Christ. So, grab your gear—let's level up your digital game with some godly wisdom and killer strategies!

Chapter 22
God > Game: Playing for a Bigger Purpose

PSALM 16:11 (NIV)

"You make known to me the path of life; you will fill me with joy in your presence, with eternal pleasures at your right hand."

Ah, gaming—the virtual realm where dragons are slain, races are won, and you can build empires from scratch. Pretty epic, right? Gaming is more than just a hobby; it's a culture, a community, and for some, almost a way of life. It's where you might feel most at home, battling it out in arenas or crafting peaceful havens in sandbox games. But here's something mind-blowing: did you know that the thrill you get from gaming, that rush of excitement and joy, has roots that go way deeper than the digital world? Yep, God actually wired us for adventure, creativity, and skill-building. These elements reflect God's own nature—He's the original Creator, adventurer, and master strategist, after all.

So, if you think gaming is epic, God is like a gazillion times more epic than that. In Psalm 16:11, it says that with God, we get tons of joy and endless pleasure. Imagine the rush when you conquer an enemy—check. The feeling when you win with your pals—check. A world waiting for us that's way better than anything we see outside—absolutely. Why not go to the source of all that joy, adventure, and thrill? Trust me, you won't regret it. God's got the best adventures waiting for you!

But as awesome as gaming is, it's got its pitfalls. Ever heard of too much of a good thing? That's where setting boundaries comes into play. Gaming should be a part of your life, not the whole story. It's important to balance screen time with face-to-face time. Like, it's cool to conquer virtual worlds, but don't forget to conquer your homework, spend time with family, or kick around a soccer ball with friends in real life. Remember, moderation is key. Just like too much candy can lead to a mega stomach ache, too much gaming can lead to a sort of brain ache, where real life starts to feel like a drag.

"Chill out, dude. It's just gaming." Yeah, I get it. But actually, the Bible has some real warnings about finding God boring compared to entertainment. That's because it's not true. God is epic, and if we don't feel that way, maybe gaming or any entertainment has blinded us to how awesome He is. Sometimes, the real battles aren't in the digital world but in your heart and your desires. That's where the real battlefield is.

Now, when you're gaming with friends, think of it as a mini-mission field. It's a chance to show what being a Christian looks like in the gaming community. This means playing fair, being respectful to other players, and steering clear of games that promote stuff that doesn't really jive with your faith—like unnecessary violence or negative stereotypes. Choose games that are not just fun but also good for your growth as a person. It's about making choices that reflect who you are and whose you are.

Gaming, when done right, can be a powerful way to connect, unwind, and even witness through your actions. So, game on, warriors of faith! Just remember who's really the Game Master of your life.

***

Prayer

Dear God, thank You for the fun and creativity I find in gaming. Help me to enjoy this hobby in a way that honors You, balancing my time wisely and showing kindness and respect to others I play with. Guide me to make choices in my gaming that helps me show that Jesus is my ultimate treasure. Amen.

***

Role-Playing Scenarios

Let's practice balancing gaming with other important aspects of life. Pair up and choose one of these scenarios to role-play:

Scenario 1: "You have a big project due tomorrow, but you really want to finish a game level. What do you do?"

Scenario 2: "Your friends are playing online, but your family wants to have dinner together. How do you handle it?"

Scenario 3: "You come across a game that has content that doesn't align with your faith. What choice do you make?"

After role-playing, come together and talk about it:

How did you handle balancing gaming and responsibilities?

What strategies can help you keep a healthy balance?

How can you make sure your gaming time reflects your faith?

Set Personal Boundaries

On a piece of paper, write down some personal boundaries for gaming. Use these prompts to help:

"I will limit my gaming to ____ hours a day."

"I will make sure to complete my homework/chores before gaming."

"I will choose games that are fun and align with my faith."

Skill check

> How can you make sure that your life's biggest adventure is following God, even when gaming is super fun? What's one way you can balance your gaming with spending time with God and others?

....

....

....

....

Save Your Game Plan

....

....

....

....

Chapter 23
Social Media Smarts: Sharing with Wisdom

Ephesians 4:29 (NIV)

"Do not let any unwholesome talk come out of your mouths, but only what is helpful for building others up according to their needs, that it may benefit those who listen."

Hey, ever wonder why social media can feel as addictive as that last boss fight you just can't seem to beat? It's because these platforms are designed to keep us scrolling, posting, and liking non-stop. But just like any epic game, the realm of social media comes with its own set of challenges and boss-level bad guys. Navigating it wisely means understanding both the power-ups and the pitfalls it presents.

Let's start with the basics. Social media can be an awesome way to connect, share, and learn. It's like having a teleporter that zaps you to different places, cultures, and communities all from the comfort of your couch. You can keep up with friends, share your latest art project, or catch up on the news. But here's the twist—while it connects us, it can also consume us if we're not careful. Ever found yourself scrolling endlessly, feeling a bit down because everyone else's life looks more exciting than yours? That's no accident. These platforms are crafted to make you crave more likes, more shares, more every-thing. It's important to remember that behind every perfect post, there's a real person who probably took twenty selfies before finding one they liked.

Now, let's talk about sharing with discretion. Think of your posts like permanent digital tattoos. Once they're out there, they're super hard to erase. Before you hit 'share,' take a pause. Ask yourself if your post is true (factually true), helpful (does it build someone up?), and kind (maybe it's best to DM them directly). Are you actually angry when you're posting it? (Try not to do that). Would you be cool with your grandma or your future boss seeing it? It's not just about avoiding trouble; it's about being a positive force in your digital world. Your words and images have power. They can lift someone up or tear them down. I'm sure you'd feel terrible if you got a bad post about you. As Ephesians 4:29 encourages, be the kind of player who builds up the team, not the one who spams the chat with trash talk.

Privacy settings are like the armor in your social media toolkit. They can protect you from trolls and data thieves lurking in the shadows. Dive into those settings and make sure you understand who can see what you post, who can share your content, and what info you're really giving away when you join new platforms. It's like checking the gear stats before heading into battle—know what you're working with, and make sure it's guarding you well.

Now, here's where you can really shine—using social media for positive vibes. Imagine your feed as your own personal broadcasting channel. What do you want to share with the world? Uplifting messages, cool Bible verses, or support for your friends can all make a huge impact. It's about being a light in the sometimes murky world of the internet. Pray over your tweets and posts. Ask God to speak to the person reading it. Share Bible verses that show God's beauty, faithfulness, power, and so much more. There's an infinite amount of goodness you can know about God and share. You have the power to set the tone for your corner of the digital world—let it shine brightly for Jesus. So next time you log in, remember that you're in charge of your digital footprint. Make it count for something great.

Prayer

Dear God, thank You for the connections and opportunities that social media provides. Help me to use it wisely, sharing with kindness, respect, and integrity. Guide me to reflect Your love in my posts and interactions, always being mindful of the impact my words and actions can have on others. Amen.

***

Create a "Wise Sharing" Checklist

On a piece of paper, create a checklist of questions to ask before posting on social media. Here are some ideas:

Is it true?

Is it kind?

Is it necessary?

Is it the best way and right time?

Would I say this in person?

Am I angry when doing it?

Role-Playing Scenarios

Let's practice using our checklist with some role-playing scenarios. Pair up and choose one of these scenarios to role-play:

Scenario 1: "You see a funny but mean meme about a classmate. Do you share it?"

Scenario 2: "You're upset about a disagreement with a friend. Do you post about it?"

Scenario 3: "You want to share an exciting event in your life. How do you ensure it's shared positively?"

Scenario 4: "You come across a rumor about someone. Do you spread it?"

Skill check

How can you make sure your posts and comments on social media are lifting others up, like the Bible says in Ephesians 4:29? What's one way you can use your social media to spread positive vibes and share God's love?

....

....

....

....

Save Your Game Plan

....

....

....

....

Chapter 24
Faith Armor: Standing Strong Against Cyberbullies

PROVERBS 12:18 (NIV)

"The words of the reckless pierce like swords, but the tongue of the wise brings healing."

Let's face it, the digital playground can sometimes turn into a battleground. Cyberbullying is like the stealthy ninja of the online world, often harder to spot than the playground bully but just as painful. So, what exactly is this digital menace? Imagine you're chilling in your favorite online game or scrolling through your social feed, and someone starts throwing mean comments your way, spreading rumors, or even threatening you, all behind the safety of a screen. That's cyberbullying. It can pop up anywhere online, from gaming chats to Instagram comments, making you feel like you're constantly dodging digital daggers.

Recognizing cyberbullying is the first step in the battle. If you find yourself or a buddy feeling anxious or upset after online interactions, take a closer look. Is someone repeatedly posting hurtful comments? Sharing embarrassing photos without consent? These are all red flags. But remember, just because someone disagrees with you online doesn't automatically make it bullying. It crosses into bullying territory when it's repetitive, aggressive, and aims to hurt.

Now, how should you armor up and deal with these online ogres? First up, don't fight fire with fire. Responding with more insults or threats only escalates the situation, turning you from a potential hero into another aggressor. Instead, take a deep breath and hit pause. (Check out chapter 2.4 on bullying) Sometimes, the best move is to disengage—log off, take a break, and talk to someone about what's happening. Remember, the person on the other side might not have the full picture of how their words are hitting you. They're firing arrows into the dark, not seeing where they land.

Forgiveness might sound like a weak move, but it's actually hardcore strength in action. It doesn't mean you're cool with what happened. Instead, it's choosing not to let the hurt control you. Pray for the strength to forgive and for the bully to realize they messed up. Always remember the awesome God who heals your wounds and tells you who you really are by dying on the cross for you. Not only that, God knows you even better than you know yourself. Those online haters? They don't know a thing about you. Let their comments bounce off you, and who knows, God might change their hearts. Deep down, a lot of them are just as insecure and need God's love.

But hey, praying doesn't mean staying in a harmful situation. Protecting yourself is crucial. Adjust your privacy settings, block the bullies, and report them if necessary. Platforms have rules against this kind of behavior, and they can step in to pull the plug on it.

Supporting others who are being cyberbullied can make a huge difference. If you see someone being targeted, send them a kind word or two, let them know you're there for them, and encourage them to speak up. Standing up for others can sometimes make bullies back down and show the victim they're not alone. It's like forming an alliance in a game; there's strength in numbers.

Navigating the tricky waters of cyberbullying takes guts, wisdom, and a whole lot of patience. But with the right strategies, a heart rooted in forgiveness, and a squad of supporters, including the Big Guy upstairs, you're well-equipped to turn your online experiences from battlegrounds back into playgrounds. Keep your digital space a zone of peace, and remember, in the vast network that is the internet, you're never surfing alone.

122

Prayer

Dear Lord, when I encounter cyberbullying, give me the strength to respond with love and grace. Help me to stand up for what is right, to support those who are hurt, and to seek Your wisdom in handling these situations. Teach me to be a light in the digital world, reflecting Your compassion and kindness. Amen.

Fun Fact: The Power of Positive Words

Did you know your words can be like superpowers? For real! Scientists say that when you hear nice things, your brain releases happy chemicals called endorphins. As it says in Proverbs 12:18, we should speak so to heal. These can actually make you and others feel better and less stressed. So, when you say something kind, it's like giving us all a health boost!

Skill check

> If someone says something hurtful to you online, how can you remember that God knows the real you, and those words don't define you? What's one way you can respond with strength and wisdom, like Proverbs 12:18 suggests?

....

....

....

....

Save Your Game Plan

....

....

....

....

Chapter 25
FOMO Fallout: Staying Grounded in God's Plan

2 Corinthians 10:12 (NIV)

"We do not dare to classify or compare ourselves with some who commend themselves. When they measure themselves by themselves and compare themselves with themselves, they are not wise."

So, you're scrolling through your feeds, and suddenly, it hits you. Everyone seems to be having the time of their lives—epic vacations, crazy parties, achievements on blast—and there you are, chilling in your room, feeling like you just missed the invite to life's biggest party. That nagging feeling? That's FOMO, my friend—Fear of Missing Out. It's like everyone's playing the coolest level without you, and you're stuck on the loading screen. FOMO kicks in hard because we're wired to want to be part of the action, especially when it seems like everyone else is scoring big without us.

But here's the kicker: a lot of what you see online is like the highlight reel of someone's life, not the everyday bloopers and outtakes. It's easy to feel like you're losing when you're only seeing everyone else's trophy moments. Social media cranks this up by a thousand, making it seem like you're the only one not living the dream. But guess what? It's mostly an illusion, a bunch of perfectly timed snaps and filters. Everyone has their off days, their challenges, and yes, their total fails—they're just not as quick to post those.

But get this: in Christian terms, it's more important to focus on the awesome stuff you see right now and thank God for it. Why compare yourself to others? In 2 Corinthians, Paul talks about these guys who thought they were super cool and were bragging about themselves, causing trouble in the church. Paul basically says that using your own achievements to measure success is just plain silly.

That's because there is only one opinion you should really care about, and that's God's view of you, not from what people think. And actually, with God, you're never 'missing out'. You're never left out of the biggest action (Jesus saving you). With God, you don't have to pretend—He loves you when you fail and when you shine. With God, you win the best prize ever: God Himself, the awesome, powerful, and good Creator of everything. Then watch as joy comes and fear melts away.

Finding contentment in your current situation is like leveling up in real life. It means being happy with what you have, who God says you are, and trusting God on your journey. Instead of always wanting the next big thing, it's about getting real joy from the small, everyday blessings. Maybe it's geeking out over a new book, mastering a new skateboard trick, or just hanging out with your family, knowing these are all gifts from God. These moments might not make a splash on social media, but trust me, they're pure gold.

So, next time FOMO tries to drag you down, remember that sometimes, the best party is the one you're already at, not the one in your feed. And trust me, the greatest party is yet to come.

***

Prayer

Dear God, sometimes I feel like I'm missing out when I see others having fun without me. Help me to find joy in the quiet moments and appreciate the blessings I have right where I am. Teach me that I am not missing out when I am with You, knowing that my worth is found in You. Amen.

***

Activity: Gratitude list

1) Identify Your FOMO Triggers

On a piece of paper, write down situations or activities that trigger your FOMO. Examples might include:

Seeing friends' posts about parties or events on social media

Hearing about fun activities you weren't invited to

Comparing your life to others online

2)Then Create a "Gratitude List"

Take another piece of paper and write down things you are grateful for in your life right now. These can be big or small, such as:

God's love for me in Jesus

Family and friends

A hobby you enjoy

A recent achievement

A favorite book or game

3) Reflect: What did you learn about managing FOMO? How did it feel to create your gratitude list.

***

Skill check

> When you see others posting their coolest moments on-
> line and feel left out, how can you remember that God's
> opinion of you is what really matters? What's one way
> you can focus on the awesome things God is doing in
> your life right now?

....

....

....

....

Save Your Game Plan

....

....

....

....

Chapter 26
Virtual Squad: Building Real Friendships Online

Ecclesiastes 4:9-10 (NIV)

"Two are better than one, because they have a good return for their labor: If either of them falls down, one can help the other up. But pity anyone who falls and has no one to help them up."

You know how you can team up with players from around the globe in your favorite online games, working together to nab that victory royale? Well, friendships can start up pretty much the same way, but instead of just sharing a game, you're sharing bits of your lives. Connecting through online platforms lets you meet folks from different places, with different tastes and views, expanding your squad in ways that just wouldn't fly in the old, pre-internet days. But as legit and awesome as these friendships can be, they need some savvy handling to ensure they're the real deal and not just some catfish-level scam.

Navigating online friendships is like managing your squad in a strategic game. You gotta know who's who, what's their play style, and if they've got your back when the going gets tough. It starts with spotting the genuine players. A real online friend respects your opinions, cheers on your victories, and sticks around through your defeats—pretty much the same as a good IRL (in real life) buddy. (See Chapter 8) But here's the catch: online, people can craft personas that are more superhero-avatar than their real selves. So, the first pro-tip? Keep it real, and watch for red flags. If someone's always vague about details or constantly fishing for personal info, maybe they're playing a character instead of being a true friend.

But what if I'm the one pretending? I'm too scared to show my true self. All my best friends are online. I get it; you wish you were better—maybe better looking, more popular, or more skilled. It feels great when people like you, even online. But here's the thing: Jesus sees all your weaknesses and still loves you. Think about this: Moses was bad at speaking, but God still used him to rescue the Israelites from Egypt. Paul used to hate Christians, but after he met Jesus, he wasn't ashamed of Him. Jesus himself was described as not good-looking in Isaiah, yet He died for you and me. Don't let your weaknesses hold you back. Let God's love give you the freedom to make real friends, both online and offline, without pretending to be someone you're not.

Isaiah 53:2 (NIV):

"He grew up before him like a tender shoot, and like a root out of dry ground. He had no beauty or majesty to attract us to him, nothing in his appearance that we should desire him."

Now, let's level-up these connections without glitching your real-world relationships. Sharing experiences is cool—maybe you both love DIY crafts, or you're into the same obscure indie bands. These common interests can be the foundation of a friendship that's more than just liking each other's posts. Supporting each other in faith is another way to deepen that bond, especially if you're both walking the Christian path. Share what you're learning, exchange prayer requests, or discuss a mind-blowing Bible verse you just read. It's like having a spiritual battle buddy, ready to help you face the big boss battles in life.

But even the best online interactions need boundaries. It's easy to let the digital world blur lines that you wouldn't dream of crossing in person. So, here's another pro-tip: set clear limits. Keep your chats friendly and respectful, and steer clear of oversharing. It's okay to say, "Hey, I'm not comfortable discussing that." Remember, good fences make good neighbors, even online.

Bringing an online friend into your real life can be awesome—it turns usernames into real faces and typed LOLs into genuine laughs. Just remember to keep your safety settings high, both online and offline. With the right precautions, these friendships can add some serious value to your squad, enriching your world with perspectives and experiences that are as real as any you'd find just down the street. So go ahead and build those bridges, but always remember who's on your friends list and why. Keeping your digital friendships healthy, positive, and respectful isn't just good gaming; it's good living.

Prayer

Dear God, thank You for the friends I've made online and the connections we share. Help me to remember your love for me so that I can have the freedom to make friends without fear. Teach me to always reflect Your love and grace in my interactions. Amen.

Safe Meet-ups: Bringing Online Friends into Your Offline World

Meeting an online friend in person? Exciting, but safety first. Involve your parents—discuss your plans, share details, and get their input. Choose a public, busy place like a café or park for the meet-up.

Activity: RED Flags

1. **Discuss Red Flags:**

   Red flags in online friendships include:

   ○ Asking for personal info too soon.

   ○ Pressuring you to keep secrets.

   ○ Making you feel uncomfortable or scared.

   ○ Getting upset if you don't respond quickly.

   ○ Asking for inappropriate content.

2. **Create a Safety Plan:**

   ○ Trust your instincts and stop communication.

   ○ Block and report the person.

   ○ Tell a trusted adult.

   ○ Avoid sharing personal info online.

Skill check

> How can you make sure your online friendships are real and positive, like having a good teammate who helps you up when you fall? What's one way you can be a true friend, both online and in real life, without pretending to be someone you're not?

....

....

....

....

Save Your Game Plan

....

....

....

....

Chapter 27
Tech Missions: Spreading the Gospel in the Digital Realm

1 CORINTHIANS 9:19-23 (NIV)

"Though I am free and belong to no one, I have made myself a slave to everyone, to win as many as possible. To the Jews I became like a Jew, to win the Jews. To those under the law I became like one under the law (though I myself am not under the law), so as to win those under the law. To those not having the law I became like one not having the law (though I am not free from God's law but am under Christ's law), so as to win those not having the law. To the weak I became weak, to win the weak. I have become all things to all people so that by all possible means I might save some. I do all this for the sake of the gospel, that I may share in its blessings."

Dude, have you ever thought about how your digital footprint can actually be a footprint in the sand leading others to the big, awesome beach party that is knowing Jesus? That's right, using tech for good isn't just about keeping your own game clean; it's about turning your online presence into a lighthouse that guides others through the sometimes stormy digital sea. Digital evangelism is like being a missionary without needing a passport. Whether it's through Twitch streams, YouTube videos, or your latest Insta posts, you have the power to share something way cooler than the latest meme—you can share the hope and joy found in Jesus.

Now, Paul was like the ultimate digital evangelist before digital was even a thing. In 1 Corinthians 9, he talks about becoming all things to all people so that by all possible means, he might save some. What he meant was that he fit in with different people and changes so that he could help more people know Jesus, while making sure he does not sin in the process. In today's language, Paul would be all over social media, using every tool and trend to connect with folks from all walks of life without engaging in sinful behavior. But here's the deal—he never changed his main message or his love for Jesus. Jesus was still his number one treasure, no matter the changes. His content was always 100% about Jesus, even when his methods were flexible. This is key for us, too. It's cool to use all the tech tools we have, but our message—the love and grace of Jesus—has to stay the same.

Creating digital content that reflects your faith can be a blast. Think about starting a blog where you talk about how God is working in your life, or make videos that tackle tough questions teens have about faith. Or get artsy and create graphics that highlight Bible verses in a fresh, eye-catching way. Every post, video, or tweet is a chance to make people think, laugh, or maybe even pray. Just remember, the goal isn't to go viral (though that can be pretty cool); it's to make an impact, one heart at a time.

Joining Christian online communities can also supercharge your faith. These digital gatherings are like guilds where players come together to level up—in this case, spiritually. In these spaces, you can find mentors, ask tough questions, and gather with friends who are also on their faith journeys. It's about growing together, even if you're all sitting at your own desks miles apart. Just make sure these communities are legit—look for ones that have good vibes, where the focus is on encouragement, truth, and respect.

Lastly, let's talk about using tech to serve others. Organizing an online charity stream or promoting a fundraiser for a mission trip can do a ton of good. It's like turning your gaming session into a mission field or using your social media skills to boost awareness and support for awesome causes. Technology gives us incredible power to reach wide and far, so why not use that reach to bring some light into the world?

Prayer

Dear Lord, thank You for the gift of technology and the ways it connects us. Help me to use tech for good, spreading the gospel and sharing Your love with others online. Guide my words and actions to reflect Your truth, making a positive impact in the digital world. Amen.

Skill check

> How can you use your social media and online presence to share God's love, like Paul did with different people? What's one way you can make your posts or videos a positive influence that points others to Jesus?

....

....

....

....

Save Your Game Plan

....

....

....

....

Emotional Toolkit

ALRIGHT, LET'S DIVE INTO something super crucial—your emotional toolkit. Think of it like your inventory in a game, packed with all sorts of gadgets and gizmos you can pull out when the going gets tough. But instead of grappling hooks and laser guns, this toolkit's equipped with the real deal—ways to handle the rollercoaster ride of feelings that hit you when you're leveling up through life.

Chapter 28
Rage Quit? Handling Anger Like Jesus

James 4:1-2 (NIV):

"What causes fights and quarrels among you? Don't they come from your desires that battle within you? You desire but do not have, so you kill. You covet but you cannot get what you want, so you quarrel and fight. You do not have because you do not ask God."

Ever felt so mad that you could practically breathe fire like a dragon in one of those fantasy games? Yep, we've all been there. Anger is like this wild beast sometimes. It can sneak up on you when you're least expecting it, triggered by anything from a canceled plan to a massive letdown, or even something as small as your sibling snagging the last piece of pizza. But here's the kicker—anger, in itself, isn't the bad guy. Nope, it's all about how you handle it.

You see, there are two types of anger: the kind that looks out for justice and the kind that just wants to throw a tantrum. Jesus himself showed us the justice kind when He flipped tables in the temple because people were misusing it. That was righteous anger—anger and grief concerning God's glory. It is real, intense but short. Then there's the other kind, the kind that feels like a soda bottle shaken up, ready to explode over, well, not much. That's the kind we've got to manage because let it loose, and it can make a mess bigger than a food fight in the cafeteria.

Why do I feel this way? Sometimes, it's because I don't get what I want for myself or my friends. We feel it's unfair, or we are afraid of what might happen if we do not get it. This feeling can make us act out, like getting mad or saying mean things. That just makes you feel worse because you feel guilty afterward. Then it gets worse, like a snowball. Imagine a tiny snowball rolling down a hill. It picks up more snow and gets bigger and bigger. What started as something small gets massive, and before you know it, you're swamped.

So, take a breath, slow down, and think. Think about why it feels unfair, and remember that you already have the best treasure ever—God. It's like not getting a small piece of candy when you already have a big chocolate cake waiting for you. Even if you had a bad experience before, God can wipe away any hurt and heal any wounds. If things are unfair, God knows, and the guilty will pay the price. If you're getting swamped, God will keep you going and eventually rescue you. Plus, listen to the other person and try to understand their side. Why do they want it? Maybe you can help them.

Now, how do you handle this in real life? First, talk it out. Find someone you trust and vent. It's like letting off steam so you don't blow up. Talk about why it feels unfair. Another tip? Get moving. Exercise isn't just good for you; it's a great way to burn off that angry energy. Shoot some hoops, run around, dance in your room—whatever helps you chill out. And here's a secret trick: write it down. Grab a journal and spill all your angry thoughts. It's a safe place to say whatever you need to, no judgments. Maybe the best tip? Prayer. Pray for yourself to remember God's goodness, power, and fairness, and then pray for the other person. It says right there in James 4:1-2, we should ask God.

But what else does the Good Book say? Ephesians 4:26-27 tells us, "In your anger do not sin": don't let the sun go down while you are still angry, and do not give the devil a foothold. That's like saying, don't let those angry bugs bite, or they'll breed a whole lot of trouble. Deal with your anger before it deals with you.

Managing anger isn't about never getting mad; it's about handling it in a way that doesn't lead to epic fails. So equip yourself with these strategies, and you'll be ready to take on those fiery dragons of anger like the brave knight you are. Keep your cool, use your tools, and turn that beast of anger into a force for good. Channel your anger to fight the real dragons of injustice and be a hero for the weak.

Prayer

Dear Jesus, when I feel anger rising within me, help me to remember Your love for me. Teach me to pause, remember your goodness, seek your guidance, and respond with calmness and compassion. Show me how to turn my anger into understanding and to handle conflicts in a way that honors You. Amen.

Role-Playing Scenarios

Role-play a scenario where you start to feel angry and use what you learned to manage your anger. (breathe, pray, talk, journal, move)

Scenarios:

"You lost a game you were really excited about."

"A friend said something that hurt your feelings."

"You were blamed for something you didn't do."

"Your sibling borrowed something without asking and broke it."

"You got a lower grade on a test than you expected."

"Someone cut in front of you in line."

"Your plans were canceled last minute."

"Your parents said no to something you really wanted."

"You had to share your favorite snack, and there wasn't enough."

"Someone interrupted you while you were talking."

Skill check

When you feel angry, like you're about to explode, how can you stop and remember that God's got something way better for you? What's one way you can handle your anger so it doesn't lead to a big mess?

....

....

....

....

Save Your Game Plan

....

....

....

....

Chapter 29
Down but Not Out: Finding Comfort in Scripture

Revelation 21:4 (NIV)

"He will wipe every tear from their eyes. There will be no more death or mourning or crying or pain, for the old order of things has passed away."

Let's get real for a sec—life isn't always sunshine and epic win streaks. Sometimes, it's more like wandering through a low level where every step feels like a drag. Sadness, dude, it's part of the game. Whether it's a bad day, a lost game, or something way heavier, like a family issue or a friend moving away, those feelings are legit. And guess what? The Bible totally gets it. The Psalms are like a playlist of life's ups and downs, with tracks that hit all the feels—from sky-high joys to rock-bottom blues. King David, he didn't hold back. He let out all his sadness, frustration, and even anger, pouring it all into those ancient texts. He showed us it's okay to cry, to shout, to feel. So, when the sad days roll in, especially when it does not seem to stop, remember, you're in good company.

Now, dealing with the tough stuff isn't just about getting through it; it's about growing through it. Think about it—when you're leveling up in a game, isn't it the toughest levels that teach you the most? The same goes for life. James 1:2-4 talks about considering it pure joy when you face trials because these tough times are training you, building up your endurance, making you complete. It's not about the suffering itself but what you're gaining from it—a greater trust and love for God, patience, resilience, and empathy for others who might be going through their own tough levels.

And hey, let's talk about the ultimate role model—Jesus. He knew all about suffering. Isaiah 53:3-5 describes Him as a man of sorrows, familiar with grief. But here's the cool part: He went through all that to save us. It also shows us that He's not some distant guy who doesn't understand our pain. So, when you're feeling down, remember, Jesus gets it. He's been there, and He's here for you always.

But hey, it's not all bad. There's tons of hope! The Bible is like a treasure chest full of awesome promises for better days. Check out Revelation 21:4, where it says one day, God will wipe away every tear, and stuff like death and sadness will be old news. That's the ultimate spoiler alert, and it's a good one! It means no matter how tough things get, it's not the end of the game. There's a new version coming, an update that's gonna fix all the bugs and glitches in our lives. So, there's always hope that things will get better—God's got it covered. And not just better, but super amazing! All the sadness will be swapped for endless joy. There will be a happy ending waiting for everyone who believes.

Feeling down can sometimes make us want to shut the world out, but one of the best moves you can make is to reach out. Talk about what's going on with someone you trust—a friend, a family member, maybe a youth leader. Sharing what you're going through can lighten the load, kinda like splitting the loot after a tough group quest. It makes the burden easier to carry and can often bring new insights or solutions you might not have seen on your own. Plus, it just feels good to know you're not soloing at this level.

But I don't want to bring everyone down with my bad vibes." I get it. You might think other people have their own tough times, so you don't want to burden them. Or maybe you feel like you need to always look happy, or you might seem uncool or weak, so you hide it away. These thoughts aren't helpful. If you don't share it, it'll come back to bite you. By avoiding people, you start believing there's no hope, no reason for your sadness, and no one who understands you. Shutting everyone out means you miss the chance to see things differently, making it even worse.

I know it sounds kind of overused, but you have to pray. Praying helps us focus on the Bible's perspective. It helps us remember the ultimate hope that sadness will be gone, that Jesus suffered too and gets you, and that God is in charge and wants to help you grow. God wants to fill you with these truths. He wants to be the light in your darkness.

Activities can also be a huge boost. Listen to some uplifting Christian tunes, spend time in nature, or dive into a hobby that takes your mind off things and brings you joy. These aren't just distractions; they're ways to focus your mind and reconnect with the joy of living, even when life feels more like a survival mode scenario.

So remember, sad days and tough times are part of the game, but they don't last forever. You've got tools, you've got company, and you've got hope on your side. Keep pressing forward, keep leaning on your squad and God, and keep your heart open to the lessons and growth that come from every challenge. The next level is just around the corner, and who knows? It might just be your best one yet.

***

Prayer

Dear God, on days when I feel sad and overwhelmed, help me to find comfort in Your Word. Remind me of Your promises and surround me with Your Peace. Guide me to Scriptures that soothe my soul and give me hope, knowing that You are always with me. Amen.

***

Activity: Comfort Cards

1) Read the following Bible verses aloud:

Psalm 34:18 (NIV): "The Lord is close to the brokenhearted and saves those who are crushed in spirit."

Matthew 5:4 (NIV): "Blessed are those who mourn, for they will be comforted."

2 Corinthians 1:3-4 (NIV): "Praise be to the God and Father of our Lord Jesus Christ, the Father of compassion and the God of all comfort, who comforts us in all our troubles, so that we can comfort those in any trouble with the comfort we ourselves receive from God."

Psalm 23:4 (NIV): "Even though I walk through the darkest valley, I will fear no evil, for you are with me; your rod and your staff, they comfort me."

John 14:27 (NIV): "Peace I leave with you; my Peace I give you. I do not give to you as the world gives. Do not let your hearts be troubled and do not be afraid."

Romans 8:18 (NIV): "I consider that our present sufferings are not worth comparing with the glory that will be revealed in us."

Revelation 21:4 (NIV): "He will wipe every tear from their eyes. There will be no more death or mourning or crying or pain, for the old order of things has passed away."

2) Create Comfort Cards

On index cards, write down each of the comforting Bible verses from the list. Decorate the cards with markers and crayons.

You can keep these cards in a place where you can easily find them when you need comfort, such as in your Bible, on your desk, or by your bed.

Skill check

> When you're feeling really down, like everything's going wrong, how can remembering God's promise in Revelation 21:4 help you keep going? What's one thing you can do to remind yourself that better days are coming and that God's got your back?

....

....

....

....

Save Your Game Plan

....

....

....

....

Chapter 30
Scared Silly, Trusting God in Fearful Times

Joshua 1:9 (NIV)

"Have I not commanded you? Be strong and courageous. Do not be afraid; do not be discouraged, for the Lord your God will be with you wherever you go."

Ever been so scared that even the thought of checking out what's under your bed at night seems like a quest straight out of a horror game? Yep, fear is one of those emotions that can catch you off guard and make you feel like you're the main character in a spooky movie. But here's the thing, being scared is totally normal—even heroes feel it. It's like that moment in a game where the music gets creepy, and you know something big is about to jump out. Everyone feels that chill down their spine, but what matters is what you do next.

Let's start by identifying those fears. They could be anything from speaking in front of your class, worrying about a family member, or those bizarre shadows that dance on your walls at night. Think of it like spotlighting the sneaky enemies hiding in the dark corners of a game. Once you know what you're up against, it's easier to plan your next move. And remember, some fears from your past might still bother you, like that time you took a nasty fall off your bike. It's cool; we've all got those old save files that make us pause. The trick is not letting them keep you from playing the game.

Now, how about some epic examples from the ultimate strategy guide, the Bible? Remember Daniel in the lion's den? The dude was thrown into a pit with actual lions overnight because he wouldn't stop praying to God. Talk about a nightmare level! But instead of freaking out, Daniel kept his faith, trusting God to get him through the night. Spoiler alert: He walked out of there without a scratch because God shut those lions' mouths. Daniel's secret weapon? Trust in God's power and promises. He faced his fears head-on with God on his side, showing us that even in the scariest situations, we're not alone.

But how do we trust in God's power and promises? First, we need to know them from the Bible. Take Joshua 1:9, for example. Joshua just took over as leader after Moses and had to lead the people to the promised land. Imagine how Joshua might feel—a totally new job, no instructions, and the Israelites have been wandering the desert for 40 years! But see what God tells Joshua: Be strong and courageous, don't be afraid.

Not only that, God totally gets that we're scared and wants to help us feel better. Imagine it's your first time at the dentist. You're freaked out, but your parent is there, holding your hand, telling you they'll be with you. That makes some of your fear go away. It doesn't mean the root canal won't hurt, but you have more courage because you trust your parent knows what's best for you.

Just like that, we trust our loving heavenly Father. He's an awesome Father who keeps His promises and stays with us, even when we mess up. The Israelites had to do scary stuff, but they could handle it because of who God is and what He has done. That's how we face fears. We use the Bible to remember who God is and what He has done, especially what He did on the cross through Jesus.

We should read, pray, and thank God for His promises. It's about turning those fears into faith-filled requests. Here's a cool way to armor up with prayer: use Psalms as your battle cries. Psalms are full of honest feelings and powerful truths. Find a few that speak to you, like Psalm 23:4, which talks about not fearing evil because God is with you. When you pray these words back to God, it's like powering up your spiritual armor, making you ready to face those fears. Then, we make a plan and take action, knowing that God will provide.

Navigating through fears isn't about never feeling scared; it's about not letting those fears control your game. It's about turning each fear into a level where you can turn to God, and unlock achievements like courage and Peace. So grab your spiritual controller, team up with God, and get ready to transform those scary moments into epic victory stories. Remember, with God by your side, you're always ready to face whatever spooky stuff the game of life throws your way. Let's keep those spirits high and those fears under check as we power through to the next challenge!

Prayer

Dear Lord, when I am scared and feel overwhelmed by fear, help me to trust in Your protection and love. Remind me that You are always with me, giving me strength and courage. Guide me to find Peace in Your presence and to face my fears with faith in Your unfailing support. Amen.

Fear Not' Journal

Start a 'Fear Not' Journal to track how you overcome fears, like leveling up in a game. Here's how:

1. **Customize Your Journal:**

   Make it your own with drawings, colors, or quotes that inspire you.

2. **Log Your Fears:**

   Write down what scares you, whether it's a big test, a tough conversation, or something unexpected.

3. **Track Your Responses:**

   Note how you dealt with the fear—did you pray, talk to someone, or face it directly?

4. **Spot God's Help:**

   Record any moments where you felt God's presence, like a timely message from a friend or a comforting Bible verse.

5. **Reflect on Growth:**

   Look back regularly to see how you've grown and how your faith has strengthened over time.

This journal is your personal guide to seeing how God helps you conquer fears and build confidence.

Skill check

> When you're feeling scared, like you're facing a tough level in life, how can remembering God's promise in Joshua 1:9 help you stay strong? What's one thing you can do to trust God more when you're afraid?

....

....

....

....

Save Your Game Plan

....

....

....

....

Chapter 31
LOL: Finding Real Joy in Jesus

PHILIPPIANS 4:4 (NIV)

"Rejoice in the Lord always. I will say it again: Rejoice!"

Ever noticed how, even on a crummy day, something as simple as a warm hug from a friend can make you feel better, and suddenly, things don't seem so gloomy? That's a little like the difference between happiness and joy. Happiness is awesome, but it's like your favorite snack—great while it lasts but not really filling you up for long. Joy, on the other hand, is like the ultimate power-up you get from a deep connection with Jesus. It keeps you going strong, no matter what level you're playing, even the super tough ones!

So, what's the deal with joy in the Bible? Well, it's kind of a big deal. Take Philippians 4:4, which says, "Rejoice in the Lord always. I will say it again: Rejoice!" Sounds pretty upbeat, right? But here's the kicker—this was written by Paul while he was in prison. Not exactly a happy place. Yet, he's talking about joy because his joy wasn't based on where he was or what he had; it was all about being connected to Jesus. That's the kind of joy that doesn't fade when the chips are down. It's like having an unlimited energy source, no matter how dark the dungeon is.

Incorporating joyful practices isn't about trying to rack up happiness points; it's more about keeping that connection with Jesus fresh and lively. One super way to do this is through gratitude journaling. It's like keeping a log of all the epic loot you've found along the way—things you're thankful for, blessings you've spotted during your daily quests, and new treasures of information you learned about Jesus. Just take a few minutes each day to jot down something you're grateful for. It could be as simple as a killer sunset, a win in your favorite game, or that your math test got postponed. What this does is shift your focus from the bummer stuff to the blessings, and that's a game-changer for keeping your joy meter topped up.

Another joy booster? Serving others. Now, before you groan, think about it like this: have you ever helped someone out and ended up feeling super good afterward? That's because being helpful and kind is like a double XP boost—it lifts them, and it lifts you. Get involved in stuff like helping out at a community food drive, tutoring a buddy who's struggling with homework, or just doing chores around the house without being asked. You might be surprised how much joy sneaks up on you when you're making someone else's day a little brighter.

And get this, joy from God is contagious, in the best way. It's like when your connection with Jesus is so strong, it spills over like wildfire and helps you make new friends and help new people. It's like turning up at a LAN party with an extra set of controllers—you're all set to boost everyone's game. When your friends and family see that your joy doesn't dip with your circumstances, they'll want to know how they can get in on that game too. It opens up chances to talk about your faith, about how Jesus is the ultimate source of your joy, and maybe, just maybe, it'll help them find that same joy for themselves.

So, keep laughing out loud, keep finding reasons to be grateful, keep serving and sharing, and watch as that joy—deep, real joy—becomes a defining trait in your life. It's not about ignoring the hard stuff; it's about facing it with a power-up that changes the game entirely. And remember, with Jesus, you've always got a reason to be joyful, even when the console's trying to overheat. Keep that joy cranked up to the max, and let's see where this game takes us next!

Prayer

Dear Jesus, thank You for the moments of happiness and the deep joy that comes from a connection to You. Help me to share that joy with others. Remind me that true joy comes from knowing and loving You, and let my laughter be a reflection of Your love and grace. Amen.

Activity: "Joy Journals"

Inside the journal, write down the Bible verses about joy, your favorite jokes, and moments that make you laugh or bring you joy. Here are some to get started:

Psalm 126:2 (NIV): "Our mouths were filled with laughter, our tongues with songs of joy. Then it was said among the nations, 'The Lord has done great things for them.'"

Proverbs 17:22 (NIV): "A cheerful heart is good medicine, but a crushed spirit dries up the bones."

Philippians 4:4 (NIV): "Rejoice in the Lord always. I will say it again: Rejoice!"

Skill check

> When life gets tough, how can you keep your joy meter full like Paul did, even when things aren't going great? What's one way you can practice finding joy in Jesus every day?

....

....

....

....

Save Your Game Plan

....

....

....

....

Chapter 32
When You Feel Alone: God's Got Your Back

MATTHEW 28:20 (NIV) SAYS:

"And teaching them to obey everything I have commanded you. And surely I am with you always, to the very end of the age."

Ever had one of those days where you feel like you're the only player left in a multiplayer game? Like everyone else has logged off and you're just wandering around the map solo? Feeling alone can really stink, like finding out your favorite gaming server is down when you've got a whole Saturday stretched out in front of you. But here's a game-changer for you: even when you feel like you're flying solo, you're not really alone. Nope, not ever. Because God's in the game with you, always. Remember what Jesus promised in Matthew 28:20? He said, "I am with you always, to the very end of the age." That's not just a nice sign-off; it's a power-packed promise that He's sticking with you through every level, every challenge, every quiet moment.

Now, feeling God's presence can sometimes be like trying to catch a whisper in a windstorm, right? Especially when you're feeling low or lonely. But here are some pro tips to tune into His channel. First up, prayer. It's like opening up a direct chat with God. You don't need fancy words or special codes; just talk to Him, from your heart. Share what's bugging you, ask Him to make His presence felt, and then—this is important—pause and listen. Sometimes we're so busy spamming our requests that we forget to hit the receive button.

Another solid strategy is diving into Scripture. But here's the trick: don't just read it; let it read you. Chew on the words, roll them around in your mind, and think about them as you go about your day. It's like when you replay your favorite scenes from a movie or game in your head because they're just so cool. Do that with verses like Psalm 23 or Isaiah 41:10. These aren't just words; they're God's promises to keep you company, to give you strength, to hold you up when you're feeling down.

Connecting with others who get what you're going through can also make a huge difference. That's where your church group or a Christian youth group comes in. These aren't just random meetups; they're like joining a guild in your favorite RPG. It's a place to team up with others who are also navigating the game of life, to share tips, to get support, and to find fellowship. Being part of a community like this can turn the solo quest into an epic team adventure. It's about finding your tribe, your squad, where you can be real and share your journey—ups, downs, and everything in between.

Thinking of God as a friend might seem a bit out there, but consider this: who knows you better than the One who designed you? He's seen your character sheet, knows your stats, and guess what? He's rooting for you, always. He's the friend who's there at 3 AM when you're staring at the ceiling, wondering about the big stuff. He's there when you ace the test, score the goal, or just need to rant about how everything's a mess. And the best part? There's no friend request pending; He's already there, waiting to hang out, to listen, to guide.

So next time you're feeling like the lone wolf, the solo player in a world that feels too big, too quiet, too much—remember, you're not alone. Not ever. You've got the ultimate ally, the Creator of the stars and the healer of hearts, right there with you. And with Him, you've got everything you need to turn those solo missions into victories. Just reach out, tune in, and let His presence transform the game.

Prayer

Dear God, when I feel alone and isolated, remind me of Your constant presence. Help me feel Your comforting embrace and know that You are always by my side. Strengthen my heart with the assurance that I am never truly alone, for You are always with me. Amen.

***

Activity: "Tech-Savvy Scripture: Using Your Phone to Remember Bible Verses Against Loneliness"

1) Save Verses on Your Phone

Bible App: Open your Bible app and find the verses. Highlight them or bookmark them so you can easily find them later.

Notes App: Open your notes app and create a new note titled "Comfort Verses." Type out the verses or copy and paste them from your Bible app.

Wallpaper: Create a wallpaper for your phone using one of the verses. You can use a photo editing app to add text to a background image or download a pre-made scripture wallpaper.

2) Set Reminders

Reminders App: Use your reminders app to set daily or weekly reminders to read and reflect on your chosen verses. For example, set a reminder that says, "Read Psalm 139:7-10" at a specific time each day.

Alarms: Set an alarm with a label that includes a Bible verse reference. When the alarm goes off, read and reflect on the verse.Some verses to get started with:

Isaiah 41:10 (NIV): "So do not fear, for I am with you; do not be dismayed, for I am your God. I will strengthen you and help you; I will uphold you with my righteous right hand."

Matthew 28:20 (NIV): "And surely I am with you always, to the very end of the age."

Skill check

> When you feel alone, like you're the only player left in the game, how can remembering Jesus' promise in Matthew 28:20 help you feel better? What's one way you can remind yourself that God is always with you, no matter what?

....

....

....

....

Save Your Game Plan

....

....

....

....

Chapter 33
Loading... Processing Doubt and Faith

PSALM 131:1 (NIV):

"My heart is not proud, Lord, my eyes are not haughty; I do not concern myself with great matters or things too wonderful for me."

Ever feel swamped with questions that don't have easy answers? Maybe your friends ask you tough questions about faith, or you're wrestling with your own big doubts. It's like when you're gaming and hit an unmarked quest with no clues or directions. Feeling stumped? Totally normal, dude. Even heroes of the Bible had moments of scratching their heads. Take Job and David—these guys weren't shy about asking God tough questions. They wondered about suffering and justice. It's all in the Bible, showing us that asking questions isn't just okay; it's part of growing deeper in our faith.

Sometimes, when you're with your friends and they hit you with questions about why you believe what you do, it can feel like you're supposed to have all the answers—like some kind of walking, talking faith encyclopedia. But here's the real deal: it's okay not to have all the answers. Even big names like Moses and the disciples had their moments of feeling lost. Moses asked God, "Why me?" and the disciples often got Jesus' parables mixed up. King David's psalms are like a rollercoaster of highs and lows. Thomas, called "Doubting Thomas," wouldn't believe Jesus was alive until he saw Him. They didn't have all the answers, and that's alright because those moments led to deep conversations with God and serious faith-building.

So, how do you handle it when questions come flying at you? Start by diving into the Bible. It's like your spiritual strategy guide packed with info and insights. But remember, it's not just about reading—it's about understanding. Break it down, take notes, and maybe even draw some mind maps if that's your thing. In many cases, you might find the answer you are looking for. Prayer is your next go-to tactic. It's like hitting the pause button and getting some coaching from God. Lay out what's puzzling you and ask for some divine insight. And hey, don't forget to talk to some trusted folks like your parents, a cool pastor, or a wise mentor. Sometimes just talking it through with someone else can shine a light on the answers.

Navigating doubts and questions isn't about having an answer for everything. Sometimes, God might not give you an answer for the exact 'why' and 'how', but He gives you the ultimate solution to all these questions—Jesus! Every injustice, every question on suffering, creation, or purpose—everything finds its meaning in Jesus. The bigger question is, would you trust Him? It's like a 3-year-old kid named Tommy who finds poison in a bottle. Tommy doesn't understand why the poison is harmful or why his dad is so desperate to lead him away from it. But Tommy knows his dad is good, and he trusts him when he says no. Obviously, we are not a 3-year-old kid. But compared to the awesome God who has infinite wisdom, knowledge, and goodness, we might as well be. Just like Psalm 131:1 says, let's trust and be happy with our awesome God.

It's about knowing how to trust that God is with you on this quest, even when we don't have all the answers. It's knowing we have all we need through His Word, through prayer, and through the wisdom of those who've been in the game longer. So keep those questions coming. They're not a roadblock to your faith; they're stepping stones that help you grow stronger and wiser as you journey through this epic adventure with God. And when you're older, you can look back and see the awesome God who was in control and had your back all along.

Prayer

Dear God, in times of doubt and uncertainty, help me to trust in Your wisdom and guidance. Remind me that it's okay not to have all the answers, for You hold my future in Your hands. Strengthen my faith and give me Peace, knowing that You are always with me, leading me every step of the way. Amen.

***

Fun Fact: Questions are Cool!

Did you know that asking questions can actually help you grow closer to God? It's true! In the Bible, many people asked God questions. Even Jesus' disciples were always asking Him things because they wanted to learn more. God loves it when we come to Him with our questions because it shows we're curious and eager to learn.

Here are some verses that can lead to some pretty amazing discoveries about God's love and wisdom. Keep those questions coming—God's ready to listen!

Jeremiah 29:13 (NIV): "You will seek me and find me when you seek me with all your heart."

James 1:5 (NIV): "If any of you lacks wisdom, you should ask God, who gives generously to all without finding fault, and it will be given to you."

Matthew 7:7-8 (NIV): "Ask and it will be given to you; seek and you will find; knock and the door will be opened to you. For everyone who asks receives; the one who seeks finds; and to the one who knocks, the door will be opened."

Psalm 34:4 (NIV): "I sought the Lord, and he answered me; he delivered me from all my fears."

Skill check

> When you're faced with tough questions about faith that you can't answer, how can remembering that God is in control, like in Psalm 131:1, help you stay calm? What's one way you can trust God more when things don't make sense?

....

....

....

....

Save Your Game Plan

....

....

....

....

Health and Self-Care

HEY, LET'S DIVE INTO something super cool and mega important—your health! Think of this chapter as the ultimate care package loaded with power-ups for your real-life avatar. Whether it's bossing a soccer match, nailing that dance move, or just feeling great about rocking your own unique style, it all starts with taking care of the one and only you. So, let's level up your health game with some godly wisdom and smart strategies that keep you running smoother than the latest gaming console.

Chapter 34
Character Customization: God Made You Awesome

PSALM 139:14 (NIV) SAYS:

"I praise you because I am fearfully and wonderfully made; your works are wonderful, I know that full well."

Ever stopped and marveled at how insanely unique you are? Like, there's no other player in the game of life with your exact combo of talents, quirks, and epic one-liners. That's no accident, my friend. You're crafted by the ultimate Designer, and just like Psalm 139:14 says, you are "fearfully and wonderfully made." And that's not just about your outer look—it's about every single bit of you being created with a purpose and a flair that's all yours. So whether you're tall, short, freckled, curly-haired, or anything in between, it's time to celebrate that you're a one-of-a-kind creation in this wild adventure called life.

Now, treating your body like the temple it is sounds old school, but here's the deal—it's about respect. Not just self-respect but respect for the craftsmanship that went into making you. This means keeping yourself in tip-top shape, like avoiding those mega sugar rushes from too much soda or junk food (we all love them, but balance is key!). And if your doc is worried about your body, don't blow it off. Start with small steps to drop some weight, eat better grub, and get more sleep. You'll probably feel more pumped and better about yourself. It also means staying clean and neat, not just to look good but to feel good. Personal hygiene isn't just about passing the sniff test before mom's inspection—it's about respecting and caring for what you've been given.

Here's something you might not think about a lot: body image. With all the crazy perfect pics floating around on Insta and TikTok, it's easy to start comparing and wishing you looked different. Here are some of the possible things you might feel about yourself

I hate looking in the mirror:

I feel anxious about photos

I feel ashamed of my body

Let's address some of these feelings. Like, you gotta have muscles like a superhero or be as thin as a pencil to be cool. Nah, that's just flashy advertising trying to sell you stuff. Real talk? It's not about fitting into a mold; it's about being healthy and rocking what you've got. So the next time you see a photoshopped image of someone who looks 'perfect,' remember, you're not seeing the real story. Everyone has struggles and insecurities, and that's okay. What's not okay is letting those fake images tell you who you are.

And where should you go to get all the 'likes' and 'good comments'? How do we know who we are? I know it sounds cringe, but God looks beyond the outer appearance. He looks at your heart. Check this out:

1 Samuel 16:7 (NIV):

"But the Lord said to Samuel, 'Do not consider his appearance or his height, for I have rejected him. The Lord does not look at the things people look at. People look at the outward appearance, but the Lord looks at the heart."

God sees what's really important—whether you trust and love Him. You may not be perfect (no one is), and you might have been hurt by what people have said. But let God heal you. Remind your heart that you are loved and valued, no matter what others have said. That is who you really are. You don't have to wear yourself out trying to be perfect or chase the 'likes.' It won't satisfy you.

Want to know a super cool secret? The bodies we have now, the weird ears we're born with, or the struggle with height and weight—that won't always be there. There will be a day in Heaven when our physical bodies will be perfect. By then, we might not even care about how we look because we'll be with Jesus, and it will be epic.

Philippians 3:20-21 (NIV):

"But our citizenship is in Heaven. And we eagerly await a Savior from there, the Lord Jesus Christ, who, by the power that enables him to bring everything under his control, will transform our lowly bodies so that they will be like his glorious body."

Prayer

Dear God, thank You for creating me just as I am, fearfully and wonderfully made. Help me to see and appreciate the beauty and uniqueness of my body, knowing that I am crafted in Your image. Teach me to remember your love for me, and tell me who I really am. Amen.

Activity: Addressing Body Image and Self-Worth

Here are some of the possible things you might feel about yourself

Discuss common feelings and struggles with body image and self-worth:

-I need to look perfect

-People say I look ugly, short, or fat. They laugh at me.

-I want to be like the guys on TikTok; they have better bodies

-I need the 'likes' and 'good comments' from Insta and TikTok

Skill check

When you start to feel down about how you look or wish you were different, how can remembering that God made you 'fearfully and wonderfully' help you see yourself in a new way? What's one thing you can do to take care of your body and respect how God created you?

....

....

....

....

Save Your Game Plan

....

....

....

....

Chapter 35
Health Boost: Food, Fun, and Faith

PSALM 104:14-15 (NIV)

"He makes grass grow for the cattle, and plants for people to cultivate—bringing forth food from the earth: wine that gladdens human hearts, oil to make their faces shine, and bread that sustains their hearts."

First off, think about God as the ultimate chef. He's the one who grows all the food we eat. Every juicy apple, every crispy carrot, and even that broccoli your mom wants you to try. God created it all! It's like He runs the biggest, coolest farm ever. And just like how your body needs fuel to keep going, God makes sure the earth keeps producing food to keep us energized and healthy. He's working 24/7 to make sure plants grow and everything keeps running smoothly. He didn't just create it and stop working; He keeps it all going, no matter how good or bad we are. It's an awesome gift we don't even deserve. So next time you sit down to eat, remember you're munching on something made by God's design and given to you freely and gladly. Pretty epic, huh?

Now, let's talk about enjoying food. God didn't just make food to keep us alive; He made it so we can enjoy it. Ever noticed how awesome a slice of pizza tastes after a long day? Or how ice cream makes a hot summer day even better? That's God wanting us to enjoy His creations. But here's the catch – it's about balance. God doesn't want us to feel guilty about enjoying our favorite snacks, but He also doesn't want us to overdo it. Imagine eating an entire birthday cake by yourself – you'd feel super sick, right? Plus, when we eat way more than we really need, we're not sharing with others who might need it, and we end up wasting a lot. God wants us to be happy and healthy, enjoying food and giving thanks to Him for this awesome gift. Imagine if everything tasted like cardboard or only had one texture. Praise the awesome God for food!

Today's a bad day. Can I have some chocolate?" I get it; it's super easy to grab food to feel better when we're stressed, sad, or bored. It's like reaching for a bag of chips when we're upset or digging into a tub of ice cream after a rough day at school. Having some junk food once in a while is cool, but if it becomes a habit, it can turn into a problem. Not only is it unhealthy, making you gain weight and miss out on good nutrition, but that weight gain can make you feel worse about how you look. You might start getting tired, lose focus, and feel even crummier. Here's the deal – food can't fix all our problems, and it's just a quick fix. Instead, we need to find real comfort in God. He's always there to listen and give us the strength to make changes so we can enjoy life and praise Him for it. It might be tough to switch things up, but remember, God's love and support are way more satisfying than any snack. He's got your back, no matter what!

Alright, let's get real about nutrition. God made all sorts of food, but not everything is equally good for you. Think of your body like a high-performance car. Would you put the cheapest gas in a Ferrari? No way! You'd want the best fuel. Your body's the same. Choosing healthier options like fruits, veggies, whole grains, and proteins is like giving your body premium fuel. It helps you feel strong, think clearly, and even sleep better. And it doesn't have to be boring. Try making a smoothie with your favorite fruits or adding some cheese to those veggies you don't like. You might be surprised at how good healthy can taste. Next time you sit down to eat, give a quick thanks to God for His awesome creations and dig in with a smile!

Prayer

Dear God, thank You for providing the food that nourishes my body. Help me to make healthy choices, treating my body as the temple of Your Spirit. Teach me to honor You by fueling my body with the right foods, so I can serve You with energy and strength. Thank you for being my greatest treasure, even more than food. Amen.

Food and Faith Trivia Questions

What type of food did Jesus use to feed the 5,000?

What fruit is mentioned in the story of Adam and Eve?

What was the first miracle Jesus performed?

What did the Israelites eat in the desert for 40 years?

What food did Jacob give Esau in exchange for his birthright?

What did Jesus break and give to His disciples at the Last Supper?

Answers

Bread and fish

Fruit from the Tree of Knowledge of Good and Evil

Turning water into wine

Manna

Lentil stew

Bread

Fun Fact:

Did you know that eating different colors of fruits and veggies isn't just cool to look at, but it's also super good for you?

Each color has its own special power—like red foods (think tomatoes and strawberries) are packed with lycopene, which is awesome for your heart.

Orange foods like carrots and sweet potatoes are loaded with beta-carotene, which helps keep your eyes sharp and your immune system strong.

So when you "eat the rainbow," you're actually giving your body a bunch of different nutrients that work together to keep you healthy and strong. Pretty awesome, right?

Skill check

> When you're feeling down or stressed, how can you remind yourself to find comfort in God instead of just reaching for your favorite snacks? And what's one new healthy food you might try to give your body the 'premium fuel' it needs?

....

....

....

....

Save Your Game Plan

....

....

....

....

Chapter 36
Exercise and Endurance: Staying Active for God

1 Corinthians 6:19-20 (NIV)

"Do you not know that your bodies are temples of the Holy Spirit, who is in you, whom you have received from God? You are not your own; you were bought at a price. Therefore honor God with your bodies."

Ever thought of your workout as more than just a way to dodge chores or get out of studying for a bit? What if I told you that every sprint, every dodgeball duck, and every dance move could be a form of praise? Yeah, you heard that right—getting your sweat on can actually be a way to worship. According to 1 Corinthians 6:19-20, our bodies are temples of the Holy Spirit, which means when you're keeping yourself fit, you're not just doing it for the epic biceps or the bragging rights; you're doing it to honor the Big Guy upstairs. It's like maintaining and respecting a sacred place, except this place is on the move, dodging soccer balls and maybe pulling off some cool dance moves.

Now, finding the fun in fitness is key. Let's be real; not everyone's jazzed about running laps or doing push-ups during gym class. But what about shooting hoops, skateboarding, or even busting out some moves in a dance-off? There are tons of ways to stay active without it feeling like a total drag. And the best part? You don't have to be an all-star athlete to get into it. Maybe you're not the fastest runner—no biggie. Maybe you're more rhythm than speed—totally cool. The point is to find something that gets you moving and cranks up the fun factor. It's about playing to your strengths and enjoying what your body can do. Remember,

God didn't make us all to be Olympic sprinters or world-famous dancers. It's all about using what He gave you and having a blast while doing it.

Setting goals is another mega part of staying on track. But here's the trick: make them achievable. There's no point aiming to bench press like a bodybuilder if you've never lifted weights before. It's like setting your game difficulty to 'Insane' when you've just started playing. Not much fun, right? Start small. Maybe it's doing ten push-ups a day, biking to school instead of getting a ride, or joining a dance class and not sitting out any sessions. And keep track of your progress. Each little victory is a step towards a healthier you, both body and soul. Plus, hitting those smaller goals gives you the boost to keep leveling up.

Now, let's chat about the spiritual perks of keeping active. Ever noticed how a good run or a game of soccer with friends clears your head? Or how about feeling a bit more zen after some intense tag with your siblings? That's no coincidence. Exercise doesn't just strengthen your muscles; it boosts your mood and sharpens your focus. This means you're in a better place mentally and spiritually to connect with God, whether it's through prayer, meditation, or just feeling grateful for a body that can move and groove. Regular physical activity can turn down the volume of the world's noise, helping you tune into what's really important. It's like a playlist for your soul, keeping you in rhythm with the Big Guy's beat.

So, whether you're into sports, dancing, or just plain old running around, re-member that every jump, shot, and pedal push is a chance to celebrate the amazing work of art that is your body. It's about making each movement a note in your own personal hymn of health and happiness. So lace up those sneakers, crank up your favorite tunes, and let's get moving in the great dance of life, knowing that with each step, jump, or twirl, you're not just working out; you're lifting up a whole-hearted praise to the One who made you move. Keep that energy high, your goals clear, and your heart open to the joy of movement, and watch how staying active shapes not just your body, but your faith and your spirit too.

Prayer

Dear Lord, thank You for the strength and ability to move and stay active. Help me to exercise and build endurance, treating my body as a gift from You. Guide me to use my energy to serve You and others, staying fit and healthy to fulfill Your purposes in my life. Amen.

***

Skill check

How can you make staying active a fun part of your day while remembering that it's a way to honor God? What's one new activity or sport you want to try to keep your 'temple' in shape?

....

....

....

....

Save Your Game Plan

....

....

....

....

Chapter 37

Recharge: Rest, Relaxation, and the Sabbath

EXODUS 20:8-11 (NIV)

"Remember the Sabbath day by keeping it holy. Six days you shall labor and do all your work, but the seventh day is a sabbath to the Lord your God. On it you shall not do any work, neither you, nor your son or daughter, nor your male or female servant, nor your animals, nor any foreigner residing in your towns. For in six days the Lord made the heavens and the earth, the sea, and all that is in them, but he rested on the seventh day. Therefore the Lord blessed the Sabbath day and made it h oly."

Ever wondered why even God, after crafting the cosmos – galaxies, mountains, oceans, and all the cool animals – decided to chill on the seventh day? It's right there in Exodus 20:8-11, where He basically says, "Hey, keep the Sabbath day holy." It's not just about kicking back and catching extra Zs; it's about giving ourselves a much-needed break to refocus on God. It's about worshipping Him and reminding ourselves of His awesomeness. We don't just need physical rest; we also need time to refuel spiritually. In fact, we need this every day, taking time to devote ourselves to Him daily. But in His wisdom, God created a special day just for this purpose, free from the burden of work and can be enjoyed with others. Isn't that great?

Now, you might be thinking, "Cool, but how does that work today? I can't just tell my homework to chill out." True, but making time to unplug isn't as tough as beating that final boss level on hard mode. For starters, church is usually on

Sunday, and it's a perfect time to rest and refuel spiritually through His word. This should be a priority (see Chapter 5). Or how about declaring a no-device day? Instead of scrolling through feeds or snapping pics, dive into the real world. Maybe hang out in nature, bike through the park, or sketch in your backyard. You can do it with family or friends. It's about finding activities that remind your soul of God's goodness and give you a break from the constant digital buzz. Think of it as swapping game time for some real-world exploration or creative sessions that boost your spirit.

And here's the thing about downtime – it's not just a "nice to have"; it's essential. It's like giving your brain permission to switch from sprint mode to a casual stroll. During these chill moments, your brain gets to process stuff, solve problems in the background, and come up with awesome ideas. Ever noticed how some of your best thoughts pop up when you're just lying around, maybe staring at the ceiling or tossing a ball in the air? That's your brain using downtime to its advantage, sorting through the puzzles of your day and connecting the dots. It's not slacking; it's letting your mental gears work in a more relaxed way.

Balancing work and rest is kinda like managing your in-game resources. You wouldn't run your character on low health without grabbing some health packs, right? The same goes for your real-life energy levels. If you're burning the candle at both ends – cramming for exams and then pulling all-nighters on a game – you're setting yourself up for a crash. That's why setting up a good schedule is crucial. It's about knowing when to push hard and when to back off and chill. Simple things like making sure you get enough sleep, finding time to hang out with friends, or just chilling with a book can make a massive difference in how you handle everything from school stress to your daily mood. Think about creating a weekly schedule that includes time for what you want to do – those things that make you feel refreshed and ready to face the next round of challenges.

God knows exactly what He's doing when He created rest. In fact, He created it so that we sleep for one-third of our lifetime. He knows we need to refocus our attention on Him and rest our physical bodies. So why not start this weekend? Go enjoy church, turn off your phone, step outside, and see what kind of refreshment and new insights you can find.

Prayer

Dear God, thank You for the gift of rest and the example of the Sabbath. Help me to understand the importance of taking time to relax and recharge, and to enjoy the restful time with you. Teach me to balance my work and rest, finding Peace in Your presence and trusting in Your provision. Amen.

Fun Fact: Your Brain's Nightly Tune-Up

Did you know that when you sleep, your brain goes into super-cleaning mode? While you're catching some Z's, your brain is hard at work clearing out toxins and processing everything you learned and experienced during the day. This is why a good night's sleep helps you feel refreshed and ready to take on new challenges!

During sleep, your body also repairs muscles, strengthens your immune system, and even helps you grow. That's why it's so important to get enough rest. So, the next time you head to bed, remember that you're giving your brain and body a much-needed tune-up. Sweet dreams!

***

Skill check

> How can you set aside time each week to unplug and rest in God's presence, making sure you're both physically and spiritually recharged? What's one activity you can do this weekend to help you keep the Sabbath day holy?

....

....

....

....

Save Your Game Plan

....

....

....

....

Chapter 38
Powering Up Your Self-Esteem with Scripture

JEREMIAH 31:3 (NIV) SAYS:

"The Lord appeared to us in the past, saying: 'I have loved you with an everlasting love; I have drawn you with unfailing kindness.'"

Ever feel like you're stuck on a level in the game of life where no matter what you do, you just can't seem to win? Sometimes, those "Game Over" screens pop up in our heads, telling us we're not smart enough, cool enough, or good enough. That's your brain on negative self-talk mode, and let's be real—it can be a tough boss to beat. Let's dig into some of these thoughts:

What You Might Believe About Yourself:

I'll never be good enough at school or home.

My friends are better than me. I'm not like them. I'm alone.

My efforts are useless. What's the point?

Everyone hates me. They don't get me.

I'm broken and lost.

If you have these thoughts, I get it. It's tough, messy, and difficult. Please talk to a trusted adult about these feelings because they might feel this way too sometimes, and they can often help you. But here's the epic news: there's hope, but not in the way you might expect. First, we need you to look away.

"Look away? What do you mean?" I mean look away from yourself and focus on someone else. Someone much stronger and more amazing. Read these sentences out loud and try to believe them:

Believe that this **AWESOME** God is for you, not against you.

Believe the **INFINITE** God with no limits is for you.

Believe He is **ALL-POWERFUL**, nothing can stop Him from saving you through Jesus.

Believe He is **ALL-KNOWING**, there's no secret or bad thing He doesn't see.

Believe He is **EVER-PRESENT**, you're never alone.

Believe He is **ALWAYS IN CONTROL**, even when it doesn't seem like it.

Believe He is **HOLY**, He never does anything wrong.

Believe He is **FAIR**, He will judge all wrongs.

Believe He is **MERCIFUL**, forgiving you even when you don't deserve it.

Believe He is **WISE**, always choosing the best way for you.

Believe He **PROVIDES**, making sure you have what you need.

Believe He is **GOOD**, always doing what's right.

Believe He **PROTECTS** you, no enemy can harm you.

Believe He is a **SAVIOR**, Jesus died to save you.

Believe He **UNDERSTANDS** you, because Jesus was also human.

Believe He can **SATISFY** you when nothing else can.

Believe He can **HEAL** any hurt and bring **PEACE** to your heart.

Believe He is the perfect **FRIEND** who wants to be close to you, even when no one else does.

Believe He has **WON** over sin and death.

Believe He **LOVES** you and will never stop loving you, even when you feel broken, lost, weak, and alone.

All these are just a small sample of how awesome God is. There's an infinite list of ways to describe our God that we don't even know about. If I tried to write it all out, it would never end.

So next time you see your reflection in the mirror, remember to look away to God, the King of the universe. Keep your head held high, warrior. The game's not over, and with Jesus, you're always on the winning team. Keep these affirmations handy and charge into each day ready to conquer, not in your strength, but with the power and love that God freely gives in Jesus.

Prayer

Dear God, thank You for creating me in Your image and loving me unconditionally. Help me to see you, embracing my worth and value as Your beloved child. Guide me to find confidence and self-esteem in the truth of Your Scriptures, knowing that I am fearfully and wonderfully made. Amen.

Activity Attribute Cards

Write down the attributes of God on individual cards. Include a brief description and a Bible verse for each attribute. Then create a drawing, write a poem, or design a creative page that reflects this attribute and what it means to you.

Infinite: God has no limits. (Psalm 147:5)

Omnipotent: God can do anything. (Jeremiah 32:17)

Omniscient: God knows everything. (Psalm 139:1-4)

Omnipresent: God is everywhere at the same time. (Psalm 139:7-10)

Immutable: God never changes. (Hebrews 13:8)

Eternal: God has no beginning and no end. (Revelation 1:8)

Sovereign: God is in control of everything. (Isaiah 46:10)

Holy: God is pure and perfect. (Isaiah 6:3)

Just: God is fair and right in everything He does. (Deuteronomy 32:4)

Merciful: God is kind and forgives us. (Ephesians 2:4-5)

Skill check

> When you're feeling down or like you're not good enough, how can you remind yourself of God's everlasting love and all the incredible truths about who He is? What's one way you can look away from your worries and focus on His strength this week?

....

....

....

....

Save Your Game Plan

....

....

....

....

Chapter 39
Navigating the Hormone Level with Grace

1 TIMOTHY 4:12 (NIV)

"Don't let anyone look down on you because you are young, but set an example for the believers in speech, in conduct, in love, in faith and in purity."

Hey there, champ! Ready to tackle one of life's big boss levels? Yeah, we're talking about puberty—when your body starts leveling up faster than a character in an RPG. But unlike a game where you can see an XP bar, these changes come without any flashy notifications. So, let's break it down, keep it real, and navigate these changes with some epic grace.

First up, the physical changes. It's like overnight, your body decides to start changing the game rules—you grow taller, your voice starts cracking, and suddenly, you're dealing with stuff like acne. But here's the scoop: all these changes are totally normal and part of God's design to morph you from a kid into a young adult. Why does this all happen? Well, your body starts producing these things called hormones, which are like the body's internal messengers telling different parts of you to start growing and changing. It's nature's way of getting you ready for the big leagues of adulthood.

Handling the emotional rollercoaster that comes with these hormone surges can be tougher than a nail-biting final level. One minute you're laughing; the next, you might feel like you want to punch a pillow. It's all part of the package, and it's important to know that this too is normal. Managing these mood swings is key. Prayer can be a huge help. It's like hitting the pause button, giving you a moment to breathe and chat with God about what you're feeling. Patience, too, is crucial—both with yourself and with others. Remember, this is a temporary phase. It's not the new you, just the upgraded version. And if you mess up because of your emotions, remember the God who gives you grace. He's got your back, always.

Now, talking purity during this time might have you thinking, "Here we go with the rules," but stick with me. Maintaining purity isn't about following a list of don'ts; it's about trusting God to know what is good for you. It's about making choices you won't regret later by enjoying the beauty and freedom within loving boundaries. This could mean setting boundaries in relationships, being mindful of what you watch, like movies or internet content, and aligning your actions with God's good ways. It's not just about avoiding stuff; it's about actively creating a life that honors God and avoids likely dangers. Timothy (1 Timothy 4:12) was criticized because he was young, but he showed that age is not a barrier to doing awesome things, like setting a good example in your relationship with God and others, or in the way you live your life.

Talking this out with someone can make the journey easier. Whether it's a parent, a cool aunt or uncle, or maybe a youth leader you trust, having someone to chat with about the changes and challenges can be a game-changer. They've been through this level before, and they can offer you the cheat codes—advice, understanding, and sometimes just a listening ear.

Navigating puberty with grace means you're not just surviving; you're learning how to thrive with the new you. It's about embracing the changes, managing the challenges with faith and patience, and keeping open lines of communication with both God and the people in your life. It is like upgrading your operating system—it's a bit disruptive, but it's packed with new features and improvements. Remember, every great hero grows into their role, and you're no exception. Keep your head up, stay informed, and lean on your faith. You've got this!

Prayer

Dear God, as I navigate the changes and challenges of growing up, help me to handle my hormones with grace and patience. Teach me to understand and manage my emotions, trusting in Your guidance. Give me the strength to make wise choices and to seek Your wisdom in every situation. Amen.

***

Fun Fact: Puberty Superpowers

Did you know that puberty is like your body's way of unlocking superpowers? Here's a cool list of changes that happen during this amazing transformation:

Growth Spurts: Get ready to grow taller really fast. You might even outgrow your clothes and shoes quickly!

Voice Changes: For boys, your voice might get deeper. Sometimes, it cracks and squeaks, but that's totally normal.

Hair Growth: You'll notice more hair growing in new places, like under your arms, on your legs, and for boys, on your face

Emotional Swings: You might feel really happy one moment and super grumpy the next. These mood swings are caused by hormonal changes.

Identity Exploration: You'll start thinking more about who you are and what you believe in. This is a key time for developing your own identity.

Increased Independence: You'll want to do more things on your own and make your own decisions.

More Complex Thinking: Your brain develops the ability to think more deeply and solve complex problems.

Interest in Relationships: You might start having crushes and feel more interested in friendships and relationships.

Skill check

> As you go through all the changes that come with grow-ing up, how can you set an example for others in how you speak, act, and live out your faith? What's one way you can turn to God for strength when you're feeling overwhelmed by these changes?

....

....

....

....

Save Your Game Plan

....

....

....

....

Walking the Walk

WELL DONE, YOU'VE MADE it to the last chapter! We're wrapping things up with some cool discussions on kindness, serving, dealing with money, and even high school. All the cool pro tips to keep you at the top of your game.

So, buckle up, buddy, because we're about to start a kindness campaign that's going to level up your game in ways you never imagined! This isn't about huge gestures or viral videos; it's about the small, everyday actions that can spread goodness through your world. Let's dive into how a little kindness isn't just nice—it's a game-changer.

Chapter 40
Kindness Quest: Small Acts, Big Wins

EPHESIANS 4:32 (NIV)

"Be kind and compassionate to one another, forgiving each other, just as in Christ God forgave you."

Think about the last time someone did something kind for you—maybe a friend shared their snack when you forgot yours, or someone shot you an encouraging smile on a rough day. Felt like finding a hidden power-up in a tough level, right? Now, imagine you could be that hero in someone else's day-to-day quests. That's what we're aiming for. And guess what? There's a dude in the Bible who was an absolute boss at this—yep, the Good Samaritan. This guy stumbled upon a total stranger who'd been beaten up and left on the side of the road. While others passed by, the Good Samaritan stopped, helped him out, and even paid for his recovery. Talk about next-level kindness!

What's wild is that the injured guy wasn't his friend, didn't owe him money, and wasn't even from the same social circle. This act of kindness was a freebie, no strings attached. Why? Because being kind isn't just about being nice—it's about doing the right thing, even when it's tough, even when it costs us, and even when the person can't pay us back. It's about putting ourselves in the other person's shoes and loving our neighbors as we love ourselves, just like the Good Samaritan story teaches us.

What's wild is that the injured guy wasn't his friend, didn't owe him money, and wasn't even from the same social circle. This act of kindness was a freebie, no strings attached. Why? Because being kind isn't just about being nice—it's about doing the right thing, even when it's tough, even when it costs us, and even when the person can't pay us back. Imagine if you were in their shoes—like, what if you were the one who got hurt and needed help? You'd want someone to care about you, right? It's about putting ourselves in the other person's place and thinking about how we'd feel if we were them. That's what loving our neighbors as we love ourselves means, just like the Good Samaritan story teaches us.

It's kind of like how those inspiring videos on YouTube go viral when someone helps the poor. Those kind acts really touch our hearts because they change people's lives without asking for anything back. It's how God rolls, too—He's kind to us without checking our scoreboards or expecting payback, and He loves it when we spread that vibe around. But remember, God is even better than any person because He's the original source of all kindness. Jesus is the perfect example of kindness. He knows what it's like to feel pain and sadness because He lived as a human, just like us. When we cry out to Him, His heart longs to help us, and He is willing to do so and continues to do so, even right now. Isn't that awesome?

Now, showing kindness doesn't just make others' day—it shines a spotlight on your faith. It's like wearing your team jersey with pride, showing which team you play for. Every act of kindness is like a mini-trailer of God's love—a sneak peek into how cool following Him can be. And you never know, your kindness might just be the nudge someone needed to check out what this whole Jesus thing is all about.

Prayer

Dear Lord, thank You for the power of kindness and the difference it can make. Help me to see opportunities for small acts of kindness each day and to act on them with love. Teach me that even the smallest gesture can have a big impact, spreading Your love and light to those around me. Amen

Kindness Quest

Alright, here's your mission, should you choose to accept it: this week, aim to do at least three random acts of kindness. Nothing fancy—just simple, genuine moments of being a bro. Help someone out, throw a compliment their way, or share something of yours. Keep track in your kindness journal and watch how these acts not only change the atmosphere around you but how they turbocharge your own faith and happiness. You're in the business of making days brighter, one stealthy ninja move at a time. Ready to make some waves with kindness? Let's do this and watch the ripple effects transform your world!

Skill check

> When have you experienced kindness from someone that made a big impact on your day? How can you show that same kind of love and forgiveness to others, even when it's tough, just like Jesus does for us?

....

....

....

....

Save Your Game Plan

....

....

....

....

Chapter 41
Squad Support: Serving Others Like Jesus

JOHN 13:14-15 (NIV)

"Now that I, your Lord and Teacher, have washed your feet, you also should wash one another's feet. I have set you an example that you should do as I have done for you."

Imagine if the coolest person you knew, someone with all the clout, suddenly showed up at your house and instead of chilling on your comfiest couch, decided to scrub your muddy, stinky sneakers clean. Kind of mind-blowing, right? Well, that's pretty close to what Jesus did when He washed His disciples' feet. Back in His day, washing someone's feet was a job for the lowest servant, not the leader of the pack. But there He was, the King of Kings, towel in hand, cleaning off road dust and who knows what else from His friends' feet. It wasn't just about the dirt; it was a lesson in humility and service that flipped the script on what true greatness really looks like.

So, why does this matter to you? Because being like Jesus means serving isn't just something we do—it's part of who we are. It's about seeing a need and filling it, not because we'll get props or because it's someone's birthday, but because we're wired and called to lend a hand. Think about it. Maybe there's an elderly neighbor who struggles with her yard. Imagine how stoked she'd be if you and your buddies spent an afternoon mowing and cleaning up her space. Or what about the local food bank that's always in need of extra hands? Volunteering a few hours can make a huge difference in how many families get the help they need. Plus, it's a killer way to make real connections. Friendships forged while serving have a way of sticking because you've seen each other at your best—giving back and making a difference.

Now, you might wonder, what's in it for me? Here's the scoop: helping others doesn't just make their lives better; it changes us too. It builds character like nothing else, teaching us to be humble, kind, and good at working with others. It's about realizing that even if we have more than someone else, there's more joy in giving and helping than just thinking about ourselves. And the joy is not just because it is good to help others, but because there is joy in learning from our best role model, Jesus Christ. And these acts are not just a random one-time thing; they are on purpose and done even when it's hard. Think about it, the disciples should have been washing Jesus's feet, not the other way around. Plus, the most amazing way Jesus served was by dying on the cross for us. He gave everything He had for us because He knew it was worth it. That's epic!

By living out this service-focused lifestyle, you're not just talking the talk; you're walking the walk, just like Jesus did. It's about making your faith active and alive in every interaction. And who knows? Your example might just inspire your crew to start their own missions of kindness. So grab that towel, step into those chances to serve, and watch how even the simplest acts of kindness can create waves of change. Ready to step up and serve like a champ? Let's hit the ground serving and changing the world one act of kindness at a time.

***

Prayer

Dear Jesus, thank You for being the perfect example of how to serve others with love and humility. Help me to follow Your example and find joy in helping those around me. Teach me to serve with a kind heart and a willing spirit, reflecting Your love in all I do. Amen.

***

Activity: "Foot Washing: Learning Service Like Jesus"

Objective:
Learn humility and service by washing each other's feet, as Jesus did.

Materials:
Bibles, towels, basins with warm water, soap, chairs.

Steps:

1. **Introduction:**

   Talk about why serving others is important, following Jesus' example of washing His disciples' feet.

2. **Set Up:**

   Arrange chairs, place basins with warm water and soap, and have towels ready.

3. **Explain:**

   Washing feet represents serving and caring for each other, just like Jesus did.

4. **Foot Washing:**

   Pair up and take turns washing and drying each other's feet.

5. **Discussion:**

   Share how it felt to serve and be served, and what was learned.

6. **Reflection and Prayer:**

   Pray for a humble heart and opportunities to serve others daily.

Skill check

> What's one way you can step up and serve someone in your life this week, just like Jesus served His disciples by washing their feet? How might that simple act of kindness and humility make a difference in their day, and in your heart too?

....

....

....

....

Save Your Game Plan

....

....

....

....

Chapter 42
Money XP: Level Up Your Cash Game with God

MATTHEW 6:21 (NIV):

"For where your treasure is, there your heart will be also."

Hey, let's talk cash! Now, before you roll your eyes thinking this is just another boring lecture on saving your pennies, hear me out. Money isn't just about buying the latest gaming console or snagging that cool hoodie. It's a tool, like a power-up in your favorite game. Use it wisely, and it can boost your game to new levels. Misuse it, and well, it's like stepping on a trap in a dungeon crawler—ouch!

Now, tithing and giving might sound like old-school concepts, but they're actually about supporting your team—your church, community, or a cause you believe in. When you set aside a portion of your money for tithing, you're playing a part in a bigger mission, like guild dues that help everyone level up. It's about making a positive impact, showing gratitude for what you have, and trusting God to keep providing just like He promises in the Bible.

I mean, He's the one who gave us everything, including money, so we don't actually 'own' anything. Everything we see—our games, beds, clothes—all have God's stamp of ownership. So technically, we are just giving God what He already owns, praying it will be used to honor Him more. It's not meant to be something you feel forced to do, but rather a grateful way to say thanks. According to Matthew 6:21, if God is our ultimate treasure, we should feel happy to give—like it's a no-brainer.

Some basics on money management? Well... managing money is like handling your in-game resources. You've got to know what you've got, what you need to spend it on, and what you can save. Start simple: track your allowance, birthday money, or any cash you earn. It's like keeping an eye on your health bar or mana in a game. You need to know how much you have to work with before you make a move. Once you've got that sorted, budgeting comes into play. Think of it as planning your strategy before a big boss fight. Allocate funds for the must-haves first—like saving for that school trip or buying essentials. Whatever's left can go towards the fun stuff or into a savings jar for bigger goals.

Wise spending is helpful. Every dollar you spend is a choice. Before you buy that tenth superhero figurine or another pair of sneakers, ask yourself: do I need this? How often will I use it? Is it worth the price, or is it just going to collect dust? Making smart buying decisions is like selecting your gear in a game. You want the stuff that gives you the best boost, not just things that look cool in your inventory. And hey, always hunt for deals—sales, discounts, or second-hand buys can be like finding loot in a game. More value for less money? Yes, please!

Let's talk about saving for the future. I know, I know, when you're young, the future seems like a distant, foggy level that you'll never reach. But just like in games, what you do now can set you up for epic wins later. Start by setting aside a little cash regularly, no matter how small. Think of it as grinding in a game—you put in a little effort consistently, and suddenly, you've leveled up big time. Saving helps you prepare for the big stuff without needing to stress or scramble when the time comes. Whether it's a car, college, or even your own epic gaming rig, having that financial cushion can make all the real-life boss fights a bit easier to tackle.

Lastly, just a word of warning: always remember who the game master is. It's good to be wise by keeping track of your money, spending habits, and even saving for the future. But if you start dreaming every day of swimming in a pool of money or thinking it will solve all your problems, beware. The Bible says we cannot serve two masters (Matthew 6:24). It's about who you truly desire—God or money.

So, gear up, game strategically, and watch how these money management skills can turn you into a financial wizard. It's not just about saving or spending; it's about making choices that align with your goals, your values, and your faith. And always remember, no matter how much cash you've got in your wallet, it's God who is your ultimate treasure. Value God above all things, and trust me, it's worth it.

Prayer

Dear Lord, thank You for the blessings of allowance and gifts. Help me to be wise and responsible with my money, using it in ways that honor You. Teach me to save, share, and spend thoughtfully, always remembering that all I have comes from You and You are my greatest treasure. Amen.

***

Activity: Money Management Game

Distribute Play Money: Give each participant a set amount of play money or coins.

Create Envelopes: Provide each participant with three envelopes or small containers labeled "Give," "Save," and "Spend."

Explain the Categories:

Give: This envelope is for money to give to church, charity, or someone in need.

Save: This envelope is for money to save for future needs or goals.

Spend: This envelope is for money to spend on daily needs or wants.

Distribute Money: Ask participants to divide their play money into the three envelopes according to what they think is a wise distribution (e.g., 10% to Give, 20% to Save, 70% to Spend).

Discuss the Decisions

Have participants share how they distributed their money and why.

Discuss the importance of each category and how they can reflect our values and priorities.

Skill check

> What are some ways you can show that God is your ultimate treasure with the money and resources you have, even if it's just a little? How might saving, spending wisely, and giving generously help you keep your heart in the right place?

....

....

....

....

Save Your Game Plan

....

....

....

....

Chapter 43

Next Level Faith: Staying Strong in High School and Beyond

HEBREWS 10:23 (NIV)

"Let us hold unswervingly to the hope we profess, for he who promised is faithful."

Dude, leveling up from middle school to high school is like upgrading from a comfy bike to a high-speed jet. It's faster, bigger, and yeah, the stakes are higher. You're about to step into a world with tougher classes, a mix of faces, and loads more freedom. It's thrilling but can also be a bit like trying to drink from a fire hose if you're not ready. So, let's gear up to keep your faith strong as you turbocharge into high and beyond.

First up, high school's not just about getting good grades or making the team; it's a mix of experiences that can really test your faith. You'll meet folks from all walks of life, and with that comes a galaxy of beliefs and viewpoints. It's like being in a huge multiplayer game where everyone's got their strategy. Sticking to your faith, then, means being cool with who you are, no matter who's sitting next to you in class or what the latest trend tries to tell you.

Now, about keeping that faith buffed and shiny. Staying connected with a faith community is clutch. Whether it's a youth group, church service, or a Christian club on campus, these are your pit stops where you can refuel on God's Word. Think of them like your crew's hangout spots in your favorite RPG—places where you strategize, heal up, and get ready for the next big quest. Also, finding a mentor can be a game-changer. This is someone who's run the high school gauntlet before and kept their faith strong through all the boss battles. They can share pro-tips, offer a listening ear, and cheer you on when the going gets tough.

Let's talk long-term goals. Setting these isn't just about deciding your career or college major—it's about figuring out the kind of person you want to be. What traits do you want to level up? Kindness, courage, faithfulness? Setting spiritual goals keeps your game focused. It's like setting waypoints in your adventure map so you don't get lost in side quests that don't really matter. Planning steps to achieve these goals might include daily prayer, joining Bible studies, or serving in community projects. Each step doesn't just move you forward; it builds your character from the inside out.

Hearing from older teens who've navigated this terrain can be super inspiring. Imagine hearing from a senior who balanced being a soccer team captain with leading a Bible study. Or a college freshman who volunteers at a food bank between classes. These stories aren't just cool anecdotes; they're real-life proof that keeping faith through high school is not only possible but also totally rewarding. They show that your high school years can be about more than survival; they can be about thriving in your faith and helping others do the same.

Prayer

Dear God, as I look ahead to high school and beyond, help me to stay strong in my faith. Guide me through the challenges and changes, reminding me to rely on Your strength and wisdom. Keep me grounded in Your love, so I can continue to grow in my faith and be a light to others. Amen.

Real Talk, Real Faith

Alright, let's get real for a sec. High school will throw curveballs. There'll be days when your faith feels like a tiny flame in a windstorm. But remember, even the smallest light can pierce through the darkest night. Those moments you choose faith over fear, community over isolation, and love over indifference? They add up. They make you more than just a survivor; they make you a light-bringer. So, as you gear up for this next big adventure, pack your faith, your courage, and your best intentions. Stay connected, find mentors, set goals, and soak in those real-life testimonies. You're stepping into a bigger world, but guess what? You're ready, and you're not going alone. God's with you every step of the way, and so is your crew. Let's do this, future world changer!

***

Skill check

As you get ready to jump into high school, how can you stay strong in your faith, even with all the new stuff coming your way? What's one goal you can set to keep your eyes on God while you level up in this new adventure?

....

....

....

....

Save Your Game Plan

....

....

....

....

Conclusion

HEY THERE, CHAMP! YOU'VE just sprinted through the last page of our epic quest together in "Totally Awesome Devotional for Preteen Boys." Man, what a ride, right? From stacking up those building blocks of faith to juggling the dodgeballs life throws at you, we've covered some ground! So, let's park our skateboards here and catch our breath for a minute.

First off, remember the main mission of this book? Yep, it was all about giving you the tools and know-how to tackle life's gnarly challenges with a hefty dose of faith, cool Bible lessons, and some fun interactive content. We kicked things off by diving into the biggies of Christianity—creation, sin and forgiveness, Jesus our savior, the superpower of prayer, the treasures of bible reading and the support of the church . These aren't just ancient words; they're your secret weapons in the adventure of life.

Throughout our adventure, we didn't just talk the talk; we walked you through real-deal skills and values for the here and now. Handling those rollercoaster emotions? Check. Building solid friendships? Covered that. Dealing with school stress, surfing the digital world safely, and taking good care of your mind and body? Nailed it! Each page was a stepping stone in learning how to live out Jesus' teachings in the everyday hustle.

But, as you know, this isn't just about getting through each day—it's about making those days count. We talked about how tossing small pebbles of kindness creates big ripples, how serving others is seriously cool, and even Godly advice on money. Living out your faith isn't a once-in-a-while thing; it's an all-the-time gig.

Now, don't let the end of this book be the end of your journey. Keep that spiritual growth on the uptick! Dive into church and youth group activities, chat up some trusted grown-ups for guidance, and maybe start a faith journal to keep track of prayers and the awesome stuff God's doing in your life. Set some goals, both the kind you can tick off a list and the kind that shapes who you are.

Remember, dude, you've got the power to light up your part of the world, even at your age. Use what you've learned to spread some of that incredible God-love around. And hey, I'd love to hear about your adventures and victories, so don't be shy—share your stories and let's keep this conversation going!

Before you skate off, let's bow our heads for a quick prayer:

"Lord, thank You for being with us on every page of this journey. Guide these awesome guys as they navigate the wilds of preteen life. Give them strength, wisdom, and a boatload of courage to face whatever comes their way. Help them to keep growing, learning, and shining Your light. Amen."

You're all set now, equipped and ready to rock the world. Keep your faith strong, your heart open, and always remember—God's got your back, today, tomorrow, and every day after that. Go get 'em, tiger!

Sharing the Journey Forward

HEY THERE, AWESOME FAMILY! Your preteen has just completed the Totally Awesome Devotional book for preteen boys. High five to them! They've grown so much spiritually, and that's truly amazing. Now, it's time to help other young readers and their families find the same guidance you did.

To our young reader: You've done a fantastic job! Your journey through this devotional has been epic, and you've learned so much about God's love. Now, you can be a hero by sharing your thoughts on this book. It's like passing the torch to other preteens who need a guide just like you did.

To the parents: Your support has been incredible, and now you can help even more. By leaving an honest review of this book on Amazon, you'll show other parents where their kids can find the information and inspiration they need. It's a great way to spread the word and help other families grow spiritually together.

Thank you both for your help. God's word is reaching out to others and changing lives—and you're a big part of that mission.

Click here to leave your review on Amazon

QR code

Keep being awesome and sharing God's love!

References

American Psychological Association. (2013, November 25). APA review link between playing video games and other benefits. Retrieved from https://www.apa.org/news/press/releases/2013/11/video-games

BibleWise. (n.d.). Handling emotions. Retrieved from https://www.biblewise.com/teens/relationships-identity/handling-emotions.php

Biblical Counseling Center. (2023, May 5). How Jesus addressed fear, worry, and anxiety. Biblical Counseling Center. Retrieved from https://biblicalcounselingcenter.org/how-jesus-addressed-fear-worry-and-anxiety/

Concordia University Wisconsin. (2021, February 16). Exploring faith integration in the School of Education. Retrieved from https://blog.cuw.edu/faith-integration-2163-1/

Cox, J. (2024, May 26). Rest: A biblically important practice for self-care. Patheos. Retrieved from https://www.patheos.com/blogs/listenlindaspeaks/2024/05/rest-a-biblically-important-practice-for-self-care/

Diliberto, N. (2012, February 13). 10 teaching tips for preteen leaders. Ministry-to-Children. Retrieved from https://ministry-to-children.com/10-teaching-tips-for-preteen-leaders/

Doughty, J. (2021, May-June). 10 biblical keys for dealing with conflict in the family. CO Magazine. Retrieved from https://issuu.com/pawinc/docs/co-maga zine-mayjune2021-web/s/12226733

Famous Scientists. (n.d.). 34 great scientists who were committed Christians. Retrieved from https://www.famousscientists.org/great-scientists-christians/

Fervr. (n.d.). How to cope with peer pressure. Fervr. Retrieved from https://fer vr.net/teen-life/how-to-cope-with-peer-pressure

Geneva College. (2019, November 12). What does biblical kindness look like? Retrieved from https://www.geneva.edu/blog/everyday-living/biblical-kindness

GotQuestions.org. (2022, January 4). What does the Bible say about obeying parents? Retrieved from https://www.gotquestions.org/Bible-obeying-parents .html

Grand Canyon University. (2023, January 25). Embracing the image of God and navigate body image issues. Retrieved from https://www.gcu.edu/blog/spiritu al-life/weekly-devotional-embracing-image-god-and-navigate-body-image-issues

Honestaboutmyfaith. (n.d.). Modern parables. Honest About My Faith. Re-trieved from https://honestaboutmyfaith.wordpress.com/modern-parables/

Kingdom First Homeschool. (2023, February 7). Christ-centered strategies for teaching kids to manage big emotions. Retrieved from https://kingdomfirstho meschool.com/christ-centered-strategies-teaching-kids-manage-big-emotions/

Koehler, D. (2014, July 6). Cyber bullying: How to respond in a Christian way. Geeks Under Grace. Retrieved from https://www.geeksundergrace.com/christi an-living/cyber-bullying-how-to-respond-in-a-christian-way/

Los Angeles Christian Counseling. (n.d.). Life after divorce: A Christian ap-proach to surviving divorce. Retrieved from https://lachristiancounseling.com /articles/life-after-divorce-a-christian-approach-to-surviving-divorce

Lowe, J. (2021, August 30). 7 Bible verses to read when you're angry. Retrieved from https://jasonalowe.com/2021/08/30/7-bible-verses-to-read-when -youre-angry/

Marvin, D. (2020, August 28). 5 people in the Bible who struggled with depression. The Porch. Retrieved from https://www.theporch.live/blog/5-people-in -the-bible-who-struggled-with-depression

Minucci, P., Montini, K., & Palladino, A. (2023, November 12). 5 steps for setting SMART goals. Boston Children's Health Physicians. Retrieved from ht tps://bchp.childrenshospital.org/news/5-steps-setting-smart-goals

Nicklaus Children's Health System. (n.d.). Digital detox: Why your teen might need some time away from screens. Retrieved from https://www.nicklauschildrens.org/Campaigns/SafeSound/BlogPosts/ Digital-Detox-Why-Your-Teen-Might-Need-Some-Time

NIV Bible. (2021, March 15). Siblings: What does the Bible say about relationships within the family? Retrieved from https://www.thenivbible.com/blog/si blings-what-does-bible-say-about-relationships-within-family/

PBS Parents. (n.d.). Six ways to help kids tackle test anxiety. PBS. Retrieved from https://www.pbs.org/parents/thrive/six-ways-to-help-kids-tackle-test-anxiety

Raising Children Network. (2022, March 20). Healthy eating habits for teens. Retrieved from https://raisingchildren.net.au/teens/healthy-lifestyle/healthy-e ating-habits/healthy-eating-habits-teens

Regpack. (2023, January 25). Sunday school games for kids: 43 fun & easy ideas to boost attendance. Regpack. Retrieved from https://www.regpacks.com/blo g/sunday-school-games/

Reinke, T. (2017). Before you criticize on social media. In Ask Pastor John: 750 Bible answers to life's most important questions (pp. 283). Crossway.

SimpleTexting. (2023, May 11). 12 ways to engage youth in your church. SimpleTexting. Retrieved from https://simpletexting.com/blog/engage-youth-in-church/

Stouffville Christian School. (2021, September 14). Physical activity and Christian living. Retrieved from https://www.stouffvillechristianschool.com/physical-activity-and-christian-living

Thompson, E. L. (2023, April 19). Scriptures to help kids deal with friend problems. Lizzy Life. Retrieved from https://lizzylife.com/2023/04/19/scriptures-to-help-kids-deal-with-friend-problems/

Thompson, L. (2007, February 1). Teaching your teen money management. Focus on the Family. Retrieved from https://www.focusonthefamily.com/get-help/teaching-your-teen-money-management/

Tithe.ly. (n.d.). Should Christians use social media? Retrieved from https://get.tithe.ly/blog/should-christians-use-social-media

Wellman, J. (2016, December 27). 3 examples of conflict resolution in the Bible. Patheos. Retrieved from https://www.patheos.com/blogs/christiancrier/2016/12/27/3-examples-of-conflict-resolution-in-the-bible/

Printed in Great Britain
by Amazon

48097153R10129